Ballads to
the Big Easy

by Her Sons, Daughters, *and* Lovers

My New Orleans

Edited by Rosemary James

A Touchstone Book
Published by Simon & Schuster
New York   London   Toronto   Sydney

TOUCHSTONE
Rockefeller Center
1230 Avenue of the Americas
New York, NY 10020

Copyright © 2006 by Rosemary James

For information regarding special discounts for bulk purchases,
please contact Simon & Schuster Special Sales
at 1-800-456-6798 or business@simonandschuster.com.

Designed by William Ruoto

Manufactured in the United States of America

10 9 8 7 6 5 4 3 2 1

Library of Congress Cataloging-in-Publication Data is available.

ISBN-13: 978-0-7432-9312-9
ISBN-10:   0-7432-9312-6

Pages 175–78 constitute an extension of this copyright page.

A portion of the proceeds from *My New Orleans* will benefit The Pirate's Alley Faulkner Society and PEN American Center's Writers' Fund.

For Michael Murphy, any writer's best friend, who loves New Orleans as much as any native . . . and for my husband, Joseph DeSalvo, any writer's best friend, a native, who loves New Orleans more than even Michael . . . and for all of those storytellers, native or just passing through, who entertain us and enrich our lives way down here at the end of nowhere in that city so beloved because it was never meant to be.

Contents

AND LOVERS . . .

New Orleans . . .

*A courtesan, not old and yet no longer young, who shuns the
sunlight that the illusion of her former glory be preserved. The
mirrors in her house are dim and the frames are tarnished; all
her house is dim and beautiful with age. . . . And those whom
she receives . . . come to her through an eternal twilight. . . .
New Orleans . . . a courtesan whose hold is strong upon the
mature, to whose charm the young must respond. And all
who leave her . . . return to her when she smiles across her
languid fan. . . .
New Orleans.*

—from "The Tourist," *New Orleans
Sketches,* by William Faulkner, 1925

New Orleans Is a Pousse-Café

In the beginning they called it *L'Île de Nouvelle Orléans.* The city is entirely surrounded by water, and down through history its people have learned to be afraid of that water. High levees whose purpose is to protect New Orleanians from all that water border the city. They have not always done the job intended. The levee breaks and flooding after Hurricane Katrina provided just one more opportunity for a reaffirmation of their faith that water is the enemy, the very devil.

Post-Katrina, I heard a woman from the Lower Ninth Ward say on CNN that the levee breaks in her neighborhood were the work of "our enemies." It was clear that she was not exactly sure who the instrument of the devil was in this case, possibly "terrorists," but it was equally clear that she was sure that the devil had a hand in it.

Water for New Orleanians is a nasty business, embedded in the language, language with the mystical quality of calling up vivid images, emotion, sensation instantly. Old dirty water is an image poet James Nolan equates with home:

. . . we can always
go feed the ducks near
the solemn stone lions
at the City Park lagoon
and siphon off some
black tadpole broth
where swans preen
in mean perfection
and stale bread crusts
bob, bloat and sink
among mosquito hawks.

The late civil rights leader and poet Tom Dent associated water with images of evil, such as "riversnake," and bad history such as ". . . stuffed black mammies chained to Royal St. praline shops . . ." in his poem "Secret Messages," a blues ballad to jazz immortal Danny Barker.

In her narrative poem "Madhouse," Brenda Marie Osbey, poet laureate of Louisiana, emphasizes through her narrator Felicity the need for *Vaudou* protection from water:

". . . The bahalia women are coming from around St. James carrying the bamba-root in their hands. Believe on those hands, and they will see you through seasons of drought and flood . . ."

And Hurricanes Katrina and Rita have inspired new verses, such as these lines from a new poem, "The Good Shepherdess of Nether," by Andrei Codrescu and David Brinks working in concert:

. . . near the heady waters of the 17th Street Canal
it's Sunday, August 29, 2005
O Good Shepherdess of Nether
throw me a rope made of your best linens
pull me up to your thighs.

When a reporter for *The New York Times* showed legendary New Orleans composer Allen Toussaint photographs of his flooded New Orleans residence, the musician's first glimpse of his home in the aftermath of Katrina, he was silent, studying them, then said:

Good heavens, I'm getting drenched just looking at these pictures. The water is whipping my body.

When New Orleanians are not in the midst of a disaster made by water, they generally prefer to forget that water and its dangers exist, turning their backs on some of the most gorgeous water views, already making carpetbagger real estate speculators salivate in the wake of Katrina. Check it out, the next time you visit, soon, when we are prepared to receive you in the style to which you are accustomed. You will find, for instance, that views of the Mississippi River from residences or restaurants are few and far between. All those flooded homes in Lakeview were without a view of the lake.

The energizing electricity of this life on the edge, way down here at the end of the world, surrounded by all that water, is among the most seductive of the powers of our siren city. And its citizens and visitors alike are charged with creativity by zillions of conflicting ions continually bouncing up against and off each other.

While New Orleanians know deep down that water is a source of both their charge and impending disaster, however, most days they'd just rather not think about it, content to enjoy their good little life with a Sazerac and a plate of soft-shell crabs *almandine* behind the closed café curtains of Galatoire's or inhaling the aroma of Oysters Ellis passed by a favored waiter like Tommy in the Rex Room at Antoine's or taking the first bite of Ella Brennan's ridiculously sinful Bread Pudding Soufflé— conceived as something "light" to respond to the "nouvelle" craze—in the Garden Room of Commander's or watching the maitre d'hotel at Brennan's working that old black magic with his *flambé* pan, playing with fire, making it dance on the tablecloth without burning it, letting the flames soar to the ceiling as he browns the butter and sugar and burns off the rum for Bananas Foster. They'd rather be eating *gumbo z'herbes* and fried chicken with Jessica Harris and Leah Chase on Maundy Thursday at Dooky Chase or *debris* with Paul Prudhomme at K-Paul's any day of the week or hear Patrick Van Hoorebeck of the Bistro at Maison de Ville catch a newcomer once again with his comment "we serve the second best crème brulée in the city." The newcomer, without fail, inquires, "And where is the best to be found?" Patrick replies, "I'm still looking for it."

Why think about the breaks in the levees when they know the levees will break again eventually, since their cries to Congress have been ignored for the forty years since the levee breaks of Betsy? New Orleanians would rather contemplate the bottom of a glass while perched on a high stool next to the eccentric ghost of Germaine Wells in Arnaud's bar or keep company with the *shades,* as they say in *Vaudou* lingo, of Owen Brennan at the Absinthe House or Tennessee Williams at Café Lafitte . . . or smell the pipe smoke of Faulkner, still haunting Pirate's Alley all these years after he described it in letters to Miss Maude as ". . . the very best place to live."

They would rather listen to Charmaine or any or all of the Nevilles, moving to the music, body to body, partners changing casually, seamlessly, on a steamy night at Tipitina's or come home happy, covered in mud after the proverbial rainy day at Jazz Fest, or put on headphones for the Marsalis *Magic Hour* to hear Wynton's quartet do "Free to Be" or hear Allen Toussaint in concert sing his "Southern Nights" or get on the glad rags to hear a talented young surgeon, reinventing himself as a pianist in his New Orleans debut, hands racing madly across the keys of a concert grand in front of the altar at St. Louis Cathedral, playing the awe-inspiring compositions of nineteenth-century Creole composer Louis Moreau Gottschalk, who married the salon traditions of Europe to wild Congo Square dances to produce a unique New Orleans sound, heralding the advent of jazz. They would rather stroll through secret gardens with Roy Guste or read Creole novels with Jervey Tervalon or birdwatch with Poppy Z. Brite or feed the gorillas at the Audubon Zoo with Randy Fertel in memory of his eccentric father or reminisce about the Irish Channel with Mary Helen Lagasse or buy luscious antiques at Patrick Dunne's Lucullus.

New Orleanians for the most part don't sound like anyone else in the South—more like people from the Bronx, only softer, more musical. They would rather hear the sound of their voices—"Where yuh been, dahlin' "—or read the work of people like Patty Friedmann, who can capture those dialects, which vary among each of the eighty-seven separate and distinct neighborhoods of New Orleans, than brood about a watery demise.

Instead of worrying about water they know they can't keep in check forever, they would rather swing with the local pastimes—curing a hangover with the traditional Monday plate of red beans and rice at the Gumbo Shop, drinking green beer at Parasol's in the Irish Channel on St. Paddy's Day, or lining the streets to give kisses to Italians in tuxedos, the price for the prized green, white, and red crêpe paper flowers on St. Joseph's Day, or tossing dog treats to canine revelers parading with the Krewe of Barkus, or . . .

. . . they would rather rub shoulders with those they take to heart, like that sensational redhead Lolita

Davidovich, who wowed them with her portrayal of Bourbon Street's exotic dancer Blaze Starr, the paramour of crazy-like-a-fox Earl Long. And Lolita's director Ron Shelton, who bowled them over with his understanding of a great love story. Davidovich and Shelton fell in love with each other and with the city, and New Orleanians loved them back—as they do Francis Ford Coppola, who generously lends his French Quarter house for literary causes.

They would prefer to play with those who have never been strangers, such as Julia Reed, whose home-cooked buffet dinners for casts of hundreds are legendary; Harry Shearer and his bride, composer and jazz singer Judith Owen, who come to New Orleans for inspiration breaks; Roy Blount, Jr., whose rambles about the city are famously funny; Rick Bragg, who can't get his heart out of the New Orleans box; and Mark Childress, who can tick off a thousand reasons why New Orleans should be saved for the rest of the world.

They would rather scream their lungs out pulling for the Saints, begging without real hope for a winning season, or begging for throws from masked float riders, such as Christopher Rice, a float captain for Orpheus. They would rather roam the Vieux Carré looking for Lestat with Anne Rice, suck crawfish heads and laugh with one another over the latest peccadilloes of politicians and bet on the lottery or the horses at the Fairground, and tend balcony gardens, drenching the unsuspecting caught walking below when they sprinkle their plants.

(Sometimes they gleefully and quite deliberately turn their hoses on foul-mouthed, ill-mannered college brats caught with their pants down peeing through the iron fence on St. Anthony's Garden or on the doorways of cathedral neighbors.)

They would rather get high on music, and food, and each other, enriching their bodies and their souls, than worry about things over which they have little control.

I said *they*, because technically speaking I am not a New Orleanian. I have spent two thirds of my life in the Big Easy and everything I am or yet hope to be has been shaped by the city and its people and most days I feel like a New Orleanian myself. My early years, though, were spent in coastal South Carolina and coastal Panama and so my view of water is somewhat skewed. In those places, when the water comes in, it goes out. And the rhythm of that coming and going is the rhythm of life.

In the little below-sea-level, below-the-levees bowl that is the New Orleans I love, I will suddenly begin to feel closed in, claustrophobic. All that water and not a drop in sight except on a sweating glass, next to a hot baguette and a plate of butter on a crisp white cloth with small bowls of béarnaise sauce and powdered sugar, waiting for the hot sticks of fried eggplant and soufflé potatoes to be dipped into them. Not a drop of water in sight except when it rains, and when it rains it pours.

This trapped feeling gets me in its clutches and I long to *see* an expanse of water, especially from a hammock on an old screened porch on Pawley's Island or Sullivan's or Edisto, watching the waves come in and go out. Or walking my dog around the battery at the tip of the Charleston peninsula and stopping to stare out to sea. When the pull of the tidewater becomes too strong, I head to South Carolina for a few days or weeks.

I can't always get away when the ocean craze, a genetic disorder common among Carolinians, comes on me, but there is a New Orleans release for my claustrophobia. And it is as sweet and fine as being in Carolina. I walk up to the levee at the Moonwalk and watch the currents of the river. A phenomenon I experience there has become synonymous with my love of New Orleans. Almost always there are waves of air, layers of conflicting intensity and temperature. It's like wading into the waves at the beach, and the gentle tickling caresses of these layers of hot and cool and warm and cold are a sensual indulgence. It reminds me of being with well-loved friends and tasting the subtleties of the pousse-cafés that were the special forte of the one-armed bartender at Tujaque's, who amused us with his mixology expertise, formidable in spite of his handicap.

Each of the liquors is of a different flavor and color and density and the trick of the bartender is to get each of the layers to stay separated until he serves the concoction with a flourish. The drinker sips through a straw from the bottom layer to the top, tasting the distinctive qualities of each, finally savoring the blend of all on the tongue. Exquisite. Like New Orleans.

When you try to examine the layers of this pousse-café that is New Orleans, you frequently are confounded by layers within layers, contradictions, sudden about-faces, split personalities, delicious surprises, confrontations with the elements. The roller-coaster ride of it all makes you giddy with pleasure . . . if you get it.

The weather, of course, is a heady distillation of intoxicating extremes. We have a saying down here, based on experience: "If you don't like the weather, wait five minutes."

I first saw New Orleans in 1963, just a week or so after John F. Kennedy was assassinated. On the plane down, all conversation was about the man accused of killing the president. Lee Harvey Oswald, who had lived in New Orleans, had himself been gunned down by Mafia henchman Jack Ruby. People were still in shock. It struck me then, just for a moment, that the city I was about to visit was a place where things happen. Then the plane began its slow approach across Lake Pontchartrain, and you could see this city glimmering on a bit of land in the middle of acres and acres and acres of swamp, located between the Gulf of Mexico and the Mississippi River, and I was immediately caught up in the exoticism of the environment.

At the time, I also was caught up in the fiction of William Faulkner, his rhythm and meter and poetic allusions. So I checked in at the Hotel Monteleone, reputed to be his favorite, and strolled down Royal Street, a street of dreams for all who favor artistic craftsmanship and objects with a history—spectacular French furnishings of the eighteenth century, for instance, and cases and cases of exquisite antique jewelry intricately crafted for Creole women adored by their men. I met friends at Brennan's, a restaurant situated in a U-shaped arrangement around one of the most beautiful courtyards in the French Quarter.

Earlier, when the plane tipped down in New Orleans, the captain noted that it was hot for November, 82 degrees, with humidity hovering near 100 percent. During brunch at Brennan's, I got my first taste of the untamed wildness that characterizes New Orleans. A blue norther came barreling in, blasting us first with the kind of sound-and-light show only God can make and then drenching the city with torrents of rain blown about crazily by twisting winds. Seeing this storm from a huge window overlooking the courtyard was exhilarating, as was the shock of stepping outside to discover that the temperature had dropped 40 degrees during our three hours at the table.

That night, I walked the Quarter with my friends, listening to music. It was cold and misty and the streets still glistened with diamondlike droplets from the earlier storm. One friend suggested beignets at Café du Monde to cap the evening. We cut down Pirate's Alley, which runs from Royal to Jackson Square, the heart of the old Creole town. The alley is named for an early lover of New Orleans, Jean Lafitte, the buccaneer who helped Louisianians and Old Hickory defeat the British in 1812.

Buildings on the alley overlook St. Anthony's Garden behind St. Louis Cathedral. One narrow building tugged at me, a Greek revival townhouse of the 1830s, narrow and tall, with balconies and guillotine windows overlooking the garden. I said to my friends, "I will live in that house one day," more as an expression of my delight than a prediction.

I did not know it—there was no plaque on the building then—but it was here that William Faulkner, who came to New Orleans in the '20s as a poet, found his voice as America's most famous novelist. Later I learned that it was the beauty, the exhilarating extremes, and the easygoing freedom of New Orleans that inspired Faulkner, putting him firmly on the road to the Nobel Prize for Literature.

I do live in that house now. And I love watching the weather through the tall windows, as it breaks over the garden. And I love watching the people passing through the alley on the way to their dreams.

Most of us agree that the most important layer of our multilayered concoction, the one that provides its strength and charm, is its people. It is the blending of people that sets New Orleans apart. West Africans and Native Americans have mingled their heritage with that of the Spanish and the French and West Indians and Celtic Americans. The Acadians and Isleños and Sephardic Jews and the Italians and the Basques and the Germans and the Yugoslavs have mixed it up with the original Creoles and then been salsified by Cubans, Mexicans, Hondurans, Panamanians, Argentines, Nicaraguans, Guatemalans, Peruvians, Chileans, Costa Ricans, and Colombians, then *reggaed* and *vaudoued* by Jamaicans, Haitians, Santo Domingans, Puerto Ricans, Brazilians, Bahamians, and Barbadians.

Andrei Codrescu said in his foreword to *New Orleans Stories*, published some years ago:

. . . I had the fleeting thought that everyone, dead or alive, returns to New Orleans. If people can't come back in their lifetimes, they come back when they are dead. And everyone who ever lived here, the costumed Spanish and French dandies, the Victorian ladies of Kate Chopin's age, the whores and ruffians, and the poets, are still here. In a city like New Orleans, built for human beings in the age before cars, it's possible to move about the streets with ease and there is plenty of room for everyone.

There has been room for everyone and the blending has produced strange and wonderful variations on cultural themes.

The best Italian crooner since Frank Sinatra is Harry Connick, Jr., an Irishman from New Orleans, and the hottest Latin music in town is by Los Hombres Calientes, led by the latest Afro-American trumpet-playing jazz sensation, Irvin Mayfield.

The city's most famous watering hole is named for the most famous of Frenchmen, Napoleon, but the

Napoleon House has always been owned by the Impastata family of Sicilian heritage. The best Italian restaurant is the creation of an Irishman, Ralph Brennan, and Italian chef Greg Piccolo tantalizes his patrons with exquisite French entrees and desserts at the Bistro at Maison de Ville. Susan Spicer, whose Anglo name is perfect for a chef, introduced New Orleanians to Nouvelle Cuisine with Caribbean style.

There are beautiful café au lait–colored Creoles with blue or green eyes or paste white skin and black-as-night eyes and tawny blondes with big brown eyes and Celts with natural red hair and copper skin and opal eyes and freckle-faced children with black, black hair and inch-long lashes. The combinations for beauty increase geometrically with each generation.

As if the genetic overtones are not sufficiently beguiling, New Orleanians are incessantly giving in to a form of benign schizophrenia, egged on by Janus, continually trying on new personae, reinventing themselves for both the serious drama and the musical comedies that are the fare of the theater of daily life in New Orleans. Multiple personality syndrome is not a disorder in New Orleans, it is high art.

Just when you think you have finally figured someone out, like Durrell's *Justine,* that person will disappear from the plot, only to reappear in a new scene, reborn, known to you only by her place card at a dinner party, perhaps, or a piece of jewelry given to her by her mother, which she always wears, or the perfume she adores. She has sensed, perhaps, that she has become too familiar, even too loved, and must shake things up, take on again the ability to excite and entice. Just like New Orleans, the old courtesan herself.

In her marvelous book *New Orleans: Behind the Masks of America's Most Interesting City,* Carol Flake explained it, saying that no one wants to be thought of as ordinary in such an extraordinary city.

Everyone wants to be noticed, as a friend of mine said recently, "to have their names up in lights." And, if they like it a lot when they are seen to shine, they are also quick to applaud generously the new roles created and played well by their friends, their neighbors, their fellow New Orleanians, and those outsiders in the audience who get it and are, then, allowed to join the players.

This layering of diverse and ever-changing personalities—the heterosexuals, the homosexuals, and the undecided; the black, the white, and the lovely Creole blends of all; the silk-stockinged rich, the poor, and the in-between; the native and the newcomer and those just passing through now and then—has remained cohesive because of a deep and abiding concern for one another in spite of the diversities, a communal sense of humor and tolerance for the failings and the foibles and absurd eccentricities and weird appearances of our neighbors and our visitors.

New Orleans, because of its eccentricities, regularly inspires flights of fancy. Storytellers come to New Orleans and their imaginations soar, taking them on trips into the world of creative thinking that might not otherwise occur. Pulitzer Prize–winning fiction writer Robert Olen Butler's imagination took him beyond the stars and back again with his allegorical novel *Mr. Spaceman*. An alien spaceship captain is on a mission to reveal himself to Earth's people, to tell them they are not alone. He has been observing Earth's peoples and places and has beamed up to his ship twelve people to help him understand human thoughts and their strange jargon of jingles, their strange customs, the way they treat each other and other species on their planet. He's excited about being at the center of a dramatic event, but fears his fate at the moment of revelation. He must appear dramatically at the moment of the millennium before thousands of people and the media. New York's Times Square is on his screen, a location that would satisfy his orders. His twelve friends warn him of the dangers but admit that Houston would be no better. And he fears humans are going to tear him into little pieces and put those pieces under a microscope and other machines and study these relics of him for eternity. At the last possible minute, while putting his friends on a bus back to their lives, the last man to board gives him an alternative.

"You should appear in New Orleans. They might understand there."
"The Big Easy," I say.
"It's just down the highway."
"Let the Good Times Roll," I say.

"I'm sure they've got a big party tonight," he says.
"Plenty of media."

"Thank you for the suggestion."

"I'd be comfortable there," Hanks says, and he winks
and he nods and he disappears into the dimness of the bus
and the door closes.

In spite of our differences we have sought out each other's company over, always, the very best food, ingenious dishes created from a poor people's basics: beans, rice, okra, fish, crabs, oysters, shrimp, peppers, garlic, onions, and filé with the best breads imaginable—biscuits and cornbread, the Southern staples, of course, but also French breads, Italian foccacias and muffuletta loaves, tortillas and pita, sweet callas, and beignets. And elegant desserts created from everyday things such as bananas and sugar and rum. Ours is comfort food even for the aliens among us.

Our differences have not separated us. We eat oysters together, we get down and boogie together, and we walk the dirge together. We manage to love each other a bit, help each other a bit, and live in relative harmony right up close in each other's faces.

One of the players in the ongoing theater of New Orleans is always the past. As Faulkner said, "The past is not dead, it's not even past."

The city has a heritage of nurturing great storytellers of the past such as Faulkner, bringing them into the fold and caring for them when they've been discouraged by taunts such as "count no 'count." And this heritage is continually renewed, with contemporary writers such as Bret Lott and Stewart O'Nan finding confidence in the tradition the city has of revering its storytellers, especially when they are young and feeling their way.

It's simply a matter of the good manners and generous hospitality of the past, which remain hallmarks of New Orleans at a time when manners and hospitality are rapidly disappearing elsewhere.

Walter Isaacson reminds us that the vibrancy of New Orleans is related directly to the layers of life of previous eras, which remain alive just beneath the newly applied coat of life, each layer of the past contributing to the present and to the future.

Just now, Walker Percy is recommended reading for anyone who would understand New Orleans and the challenges ahead. Walker used to hang out in the Quarter, alone, when he was writing. He once rented an apartment next to me and we got to know each other sufficiently well for me to be invited to some of his think-tank luncheon sessions at Béchac's in Mandeville, looking back across Lake Pontchartrain to New Orleans. He was a combination of Calvinist work ethic and Catholic guilt and intellectual twists of humor. He was a good man and he worried about the future of Americankind.

He looked upon New Orleans as a possible way back for the rest of America, a model for national salvation, if New Orleans could just finally get its act together and come to grips with the big issues of education and jobs for the poor, and expanded opportunities for the marginalized to move up the class ladder.

In his essay "New Orleans, Mon Amour," he emphasized that the heroic deed has not been the style of New Orleanians but said that, if in its 250 years the city has produced no giants, no Lincolns or Lees, "it has nurtured a great many people who live tolerably, like to talk and eat, laugh a good deal, manage generally to be civil and at the same time mind their own business. Such virtues may have their use nowadays."

His essay, written originally for *Harpers*, was published in 1968 and it is as meaningful today.

"The peculiar virtue of New Orleans, like St. Theresa, may be that of the Little Way, a talent for everyday life rather than the heroic deed," Mr. Percy said.

We've had a good everyday life together. We have had it all, down here at the end of the world, jumping-off place to nowhere, down here where the edginess of it all is exhilarating, seducing, inspiring.

We can have it again and will, but first we must face the big issues Mr. Percy cited in 1968 and which are with us still.

Now we must find the inspiration for a new, unfamiliar role; we must reinvent ourselves as heroes, capable of not only bringing a great city back, but of making it better for all New Orleanians; capable of facing down that old demon water and overcoming it with skill and ingenuity; capable of preserving the precious originality of New Orleans neighborhoods and their style, the music of New Orleans, its food, its lingo, its soul.

A wise man said to the Athenians:

> Look at the city's real power day after day,
> and fall in love with her,
> and if she seems great to you, remember that men built
> these things who knew what needed to be done and
> dared to do it,
> and if they fell short of their goal,
> they never thought to deprive the city
> of their talent;
> they gave her their best.

If we do just that, then we will enjoy once again our Little Way.

Ballads to the Big Easy by Her Sons . . .

Nasty Water

To Joanna Palmer

Joanna complains that Jules
tossed out the slimy water
with the dead roses in it
she was saving to paint
a formal portrait of death,
une nature morte.

She can dry more white roses
but where is she going to get
another vase of that
nasty water?
Joanna,
let's haunt the cemetery
a week after Easter
to scoop up green scum
from the lilies rotting

in their marble urns.
Better yet, we could hide
behind the tombs waiting
for a fresh burial, tie
a string to a mason jar
then drop it down
that well into the murky
crayfish contagion
of our ancestors' bones. . . .

Nasty water? You say
you want nasty water?
New Orleans is a shimmering
mirage floating on nasty water,
irrigated by nasty water,
nasty water seeping out
of every pore, steeping
in crab grass on the levee
like a bitter green tea
then trickling in rivulets
down to that Queen of Nasty
Water, the Mississippi,
Gaia of primordial funk,
mother of us all. We drink
her, brew her, cook her up
into okra gumbo, into
a lifelong Scorpionic
soup of afterbirths
and Extreme Unctions,

secretions and
family secrets:

nasty water,
nasty water,
proud to call it home.

—JAMES NOLAN

How to Bring the Magic Back

WALTER ISAACSON

All of us from New Orleans have savored that Proust-bites-into-the-madeleine moment when a stray taste, sound, smell, or sight brings remembrances of things past. It happens whenever I hear the badly rhymed but beautifully mournful—now even more so—first few bars of "Do You Know What It Means to Miss New Orleans?" It can even happen with a single chord. A friend gave me a CD of a local band called Jonas Rising, and at the sound of the very first Neville Brothers–inspired piano chord, I was back inside Tipitina's, where Napoleon Avenue meets the Mississippi, listening to Professor Longhair.

The taste of a particularly pungent garlic sauce can evoke similar remembrances. What makes New Orleans eating so joyous is not just classic restaurants such as Antoine's or Commander's Palace. It's the neighborhood places such as those just up Napoleon from Tipitina's: the pan-roasted oysters at Manale's and the fried ones at Casamento's, nestled between a costume store and a building-ornament supply shop.

My family home was, and I hope still is, on Napoleon Avenue as well. It's a raised West Indian cottage, at merely one hundred years old not historic by local standards yet part of the distinctive mix that makes even the uncelebrated neighborhoods of New Orleans so seductive. It was in neighborhoods such as these, more than the famous ones, where people lost their lives and cherished communities were washed away. I glimpsed on CNN our avenue underwater and felt like crying.

I was just in Venice, a city of masks and decadent grace that New Orleanians are genetically encoded to find enchanting. Because it's a world treasure, there is an international Save Venice movement. I hope New Orleans will evoke the same response.

But saving New Orleans will require not merely re-creating the French Quarter. It will involve nurturing back to health the genuine and distinctive neighborhoods that serve as an incubator for the city's music and food and funkiness. A friend of mine, Stephanie Bruno, has run an organization that restores old shotgun cottages, the long and narrow houses built of old barge planks that dominate in the older areas. A New Orleans rebuilt with tract homes rather than shotguns would no longer have the same soul.

The best writers to have lived in New Orleans were William Faulkner and Tennessee Williams. But my other favorites were two who knew the neighborhoods better. Walker Percy wrote about the savory malaise emanating from middle-class enclaves such as Gentilly and Elysian

Fields. And Lillian Hellman recalled wandering up Esplanade Avenue below the French Quarter.

Hellman titled her second book of memoirs *Pentimento,* meaning the brushstrokes and old images that struggle to emerge from a repainted canvas. You see that a lot in New Orleans: advertisements for defunct brands of beer and coffee poking through the fading paint of old brick buildings. Indeed, it has always been a city of masks and painted faces, with past mysteries and glories lurking faintly visible underneath.

After disasters such as Hurricane Katrina, it's commonplace to extol the fierce determination of the afflicted as they rise like a phoenix. But indomitable energy is not what earned New Orleans the sobriquet the Big Easy, and it has never been a phoenix in any sense. The evacuees I know talked about wandering to visit far-flung friends for a few months before heading home.

It's probably not in the nature of most New Orleanians to roll up their sleeves and quickly build a grander city. They're better at making things akin to Creole gumbo and Cajun jambalaya—which involve a variety of ingredients and spices that are blended slowly. You start by making a roux, the mix of hot oil and flour that can hold the tastes together, a process that ought not be rushed.

This easygoing lethargy might actually serve New Orleans well as it rebuilds. The city needs to restore itself authentically rather than produce a theme-park recreation. It needs shotguns, not cold condos. Its talented preservation and community-planning experts should be offered the chance to devise a land-use approach that revives charming old neighborhood patterns rather than producing alienating culs-de-sac or artificial quaintness. It has the opportunity to rebuild itself in a way that emerges from its rich heritage while guarding against any projects that would sap its soul.

Like a *pentimento*, New Orleans has long been a canvas repeatedly repainted. Paint well, my artistic homeboys and girls, and carefully. Preserve the previous layers, and let them guide your brushwork. One false stroke, and the magic could disappear.

Soul Model for America

Wynton Marsalis

New Orleans is the most unique of American cities because it is the only city in the world that created its own full culture—architecture, music, and festive ceremonies.

It's of singular importance to the United States of America because it was the original melting pot, with a mixture of Spanish, French, British, West African, and American people living in the same city.

The collision of these cultures created jazz, and jazz is important because it's the only art form that objectifies the fundamental principals of American democracy. That's why it swept the country and the world, representing the best of the United States.

New Orleanians are blues people. We are resilient, so we are sure that our city will come back. The mythic significance of this tragedy, Katrina, however, provides an opportunity for the American people to demonstrate to ourselves and to the world that we are one nation, determined to overcome our legacies of injustices based on race and class.

At this time all New Orleanians need the nation to

unite in a deafening crescendo of affirmation to silence the desperate cry that is this disaster.

We need people with their prayers, their pocketbooks, and above all, their sense of purpose to show the world just who the modern American is and then we'll put our city back together in even greater fashion.

This is gut-check time for all of us as Americans.

In a country with the most incredible resources in the world we need the ingenuity of our best engineers to put the cultural heart of our nation back together. To put it together with 2005 technical expertise and with 2005 social consciousness, which means without accommodating the ignorance of racism, the deplorable conditions of poverty, and the lack of education that have been allowed to fester in many great American cities since slavery.

We're only as civilized as our level of hospitality. Let's demonstrate to the world that what actually makes America the most powerful nation on earth is not guns, pornography, or material wealth but transcendent and abiding soul, something perhaps we have lost a grip on, and this catastrophe gives us a great opportunity to handle up.

I Am Creole

Roy F. Guste, Jr.

I am a word, a person, a culture, a lifestyle, a city. A way
to see life. A way to live life. A way to love and a way to
defend. Pugnacious. A way to fight, a way to honor. A
tomato. I have a warm heart and a will of iron. I am a
lowly reed that bends in the wind and an oak that stands
tall and wide and strong. I have scruples. I have ethics. I
have beliefs. Remember these things? I try to judge not,
but when I must, it is by action and virtue, not color or
religion or wealth. The lowest among us have more sub-
stance than most others elsewhere.

I live in the detail. The coffee I drink, the perfume of
the magnolia blossoms, and tea olive outside my Vieux
Carré window. I buy produce in the French Market and
enjoy *bouilli* at Tujague's. I breakfast at Brennan's, I lunch
at Dooky Chase and Galatoire's and Broussard's and
Arnaud's, and I dine at Antoine's. I am the intoxication of
night-blooming jasmine as I walk the streets of an
evening. I am a palette of white, brown, and nearly
black, and of all hues in between. Sometimes I am the
color of a grocer's paper bag. I am café au lait. I am
beignets at Café du Monde and taffy from an ancient

wagon. I eat po'boys, not subs. I eat red beans, not black, sometimes on Thursday, but always on Monday. I have eyes that bathe you, not watch you. I don't talk, I converse. And I set *mes raconteurs* on a pedestal, high, *la place d'honneur.*

I laugh. With all my being I laugh. Sometimes you can find me far away from home in restaurants. I am the laughing one in the corner. I don't need to meet you. I know you already. I know your *grandmère* and *tu tante* Tatine, *ton oncle* Jean, and *ton fils* Justin. My camellia and azalea stand near my kumquat and Japanese plum. My fig and elephant ear near my persimmon. My pecan tree yields pies, my orange tree ambrosia, and sometimes my bananas Foster. I eat an oyster loaf. I drink my mint. And sassafras is essential to my gumbo and root beer. I don't beat my drum, I eat it, sometimes red, sometimes black. And sometimes my fish croak. I fry catfish and court bouillon my redfish. I papillote my pompano and Rockefeller my oysters. My music is jazz.

My Louisiana Indian forefathers gave me filé and corn and squash and beans. My African forefathers gave me rice and black-eyed peas and okra. My French forefathers gave me my precious *roux* and their precious cuisine. And my Spanish forefathers infused tomatoes and bell peppers into the mix. And, of course, made salad a course. My great restaurants are older than a century. Sometimes a century and a half. My home is older than that. My past surrounds me. Ursuline convent, St. Mary's Italian Church, Café Lafitte, the Pontalbas. My street is a *rue*. My pathway a *banquette*, my sweet a pra-line. My saints are Expidito and Our Lady of Prompt Succor, and lost causes has its own Jude. I drink my chicory. I simmer my milk. I flame my coffee with co-gnac and orange rind and cinnamon and clove. I cocktail with Sazeracs. I danced at the Roosevelt. I have finished my evenings with 2:00 a.m. breakfasts at Lucky Pierre's. My grandparents were Memère and Pepère. The little one of the same name is "tite" something or other. My eyes are pools of chocolate or seas of green. My scarf is a *tignon*. My *callas* sings not to the ear, but to the tongue. And my rice is always steamed. My potatoes are souf-fléed. My bread is French and sometimes lost, but on the plate, nonetheless. My uncle is a priest, my cousin a nun. My iron is wrought. My roof is slate. My floor is cypress. My brick is soft and red. My balcony is my porch. My court is my yard. My entrance is a carriageway. My back house is a slave quarter. When I pass by to make gro-ceries, there is ballast beneath my feet. And when I am by ma mamma's, you can always pass time with me. After, all, I am *en famille*. Aren't I? And to others not related but so bound by friendship and years enough you call me uncle, cousin, aunt. And sometimes, but not always, I do know where y'at.

My pudding is bread or corn. The eyes of my fish must sparkle and the tails of my crayfish must curl. My oysters are salty and my shrimp are numbered. My mirli-ton is stuffed and my étouffée is sublime. My toast is French. My sandwich is dressed. My bag is a grip and I wash in the zinc. Because of the tax man, my house has no closets. Armoires of French walnut and Haitian mahogany hold my clothes.

No war, no storm, no unitedness of these states can destroy me. I am a survivor. I may be forever. I am Creole. I am New Orleans.

A Very Big New Orleans Family in a Very Small World

JERVEY TERVALON

Not that long ago, when I did a book signing at the Latter Branch Library on St. Charles Avenue—something my cousin Ellen Hazeur, who was then the city councilwoman for the Ninth Ward, had arranged—a woman I thought to be white reached the head of the line with special instructions on how to sign her copy of my novel *Dead Above Ground*. She introduced herself as a relative and the explanation of how we were related was too complicated for me to follow. Then she asked me to inscribe the book to her and said her last name was Tervalon-Tervalon. I must have raised an eyebrow because she quickly leaped into an explanation of the Tervalon-Tervalon, and this, too, I couldn't follow. For whatever reason my mind fixated on Tervalon-Tervalon. Is that Tervalon squared or is it Tervalon to the second power? "You see, I want people to understand that I didn't marry my cousin. We're from different sides of the family," she said with the conviction of a person who didn't want to look foolish, but thought maybe she was.

I wanted to ask what she meant by "different sides of the family," but she moved on to get more champagne. Later, I called my father and asked what he thought of this "different sides of the family" concept and he snorted. "I know her. She's one of your cousins. I bet she's trying to say she married white so her husband couldn't possibly be related. That's a bunch of malarkey. She married a distant relative."

That's what I love about New Orleans; trying to understand it is a lifetime of productive bewilderment.

I've written two novels set in New Orleans and have been interviewed a number of times and yet no one has ever asked what that's like: to write novels in the voice of your mother. I always wanted the opportunity to respond that I'm an incestuous literary transvestite. The truth is I'm a lazy writer and I think that's the key to whatever success I've had as a writer. Why work harder to find material than you have to? Faulkner had Yoknapatawpha County, I have my mother, an undiscovered continent of literary material. I remember her story about the birth of my oldest brother, which I have to say is a great tale. My parents, two "negroes," albeit pretty damn white "negroes," had my oldest brother, Hillary, the whitest, bluest-eyed colored baby ever born at Charity Hospital. She said when they got him home friends and neighbors took a look at Hillary and decided that my mother had given birth to the infant Jesus. Sure, it seems odd that people would think having a Northern European–looking baby would be such a noteworthy achievement that they would equate it with having Jesus as a son, but it does somewhat explain the power, threat, and absurdity of race. Faulkner had Joe Christmas, and I had my brother, the white black man.

In New Orleans this made some kind of sense, but when we moved west, in the vastness of Los Angeles the subtleties of Jim Crow and race politics didn't register. You were either or, black or white, and if you were black you needed to live on the appropriate reservation. Nobody seemed to notice how Mexican the town was. A friend from college visited New Orleans and she came back with the information that she kept running into people who looked like me. I replied that's because of the generations of us marrying our cousins, and it's good for a people to keep those distended bloodlines strong. I think she might even have believed me.

Bring Back the Clowns

RANDY FERTEL

New Orleanians have long memories and a high tolerance for eccentricity. As we put our post-hurricane city back together we must draw on both strengths.

When New Orleanians of a certain age hear my name, some salivate because my mother, the late Ruth Fertel, founded Ruth's Chris Steak House. But others recoil, and still others break into a wide grin. Either of these responses and I know they are thinking of my dad, the late Rodney Fertel.

Dad was known as the Gorilla Man for his 1969 mayoral campaign, when the sole plank in his platform was that the Audubon Zoo needed a gorilla. He campaigned in a safari outfit, complete with pith helmet, proof to many that he meant to send up the pols who ran our Third World banana republic. Invited to ride in a parade during the election, Dad tracked down a man whose gorilla suit he had admired during Mardi Gras. They rode together in a convertible and every few blocks Dad would send the gorilla over the side to make a show, sniffing at some unfortunate young woman and beating his chest. His campaign slogan was "Why vote for those monkeys when you can vote for Fertel and get a gorilla?" He got 308 votes then went out and bought two gorillas for the zoo, the only candidate in history, he announced, who had kept all his campaign promises, even though he'd lost.

In 1973, Dad campaigned again, this time on the promise that he would bring the Blarney Stone from Ireland and put it temporarily in the Superdome. In 1977, he promised to swim in the Mississippi River at Canal Street "for at least five minutes" to get publicity for the city.

Dad's campaign manager and sidekick was Allen "The Black Cat" Lacombe—a character straight out of Damon Runyan's *Guys and Dolls*. A perennial candidate himself, Allen's principal political asset was his sure hand at hilarity. The Black Cat was as proud of his nickname as the Gorilla Man was of his. He was happy to explain that he always lost at everything, including the wrestling matches he bet on even though everyone knew they were fixed. During a stint as the sports page handicapper, he selected nine winners one day for his column, then bet against them all.

During the 1959 governor's race, the Black Cat was invited to a dinner honoring Robert F. Kennedy. He was a candidate, so he sat at the high table in his rented tuxedo with the future president's brother. He sported a campaign button the size of a café au lait saucer that read, "Use Your Dome, Vote Lacombe." Had even

Boston politics prepared Bobby Kennedy for such a boon dinner companion?

Lacombe was immortalized in *The Earl of Louisiana,* in which A. J. Liebling, in covering Earl Long's run for governor that year, records this bit of madcap campaigning:

A customer came over from the bar and said to the Black Cat, "I'm going to vote for you, Governor; you're better than them other sonsabitches, anyway."

"What precinct you vote in?" the candidate asked and, after the man told him, said, "Well, I'm going to look at the returns Sunday, and if I don't have one vote in that precinct I'll know you're a lying sonofabitch."

The man went away laughing, and the candidate said, "I might even finish fifth." Actually, the Black Cat would have said "fif." The Black Cat's thick accent was what New Orleanians call "y'at," named for the denizens of the Ninth Ward who ask gingerly, "Where y'at?" meaning a combination of "How are you?" and "What's happening?" This is the accent that charmed A. J. Liebling and amazed post-Katrina America. Closer to what we know as Brooklynese than anything else, the brogue is probably the result of the same Irish immigration that populated the inner cities in Brooklyn and Baltimore and San Francisco in the 1840s and '50s. The dialect helped to produce such gems as the characters of John Kennedy Toole's *A Confederacy of Dunces* and Mayor Robert Maestri's query to Franklin Roosevelt when they ate Oysters Rockefeller at Antoine's, "How'd ya like dem ersters, Mr. President?" The Black Cat was one a dem.

Like the Black Cat, the Gorilla Man seems never to have lost his sense of humor. Before entering the operating room for a critical procedure just weeks before he died, he was asked if he was allergic to anything. Though he suffered at the end of his life from senile dementia, nonetheless he answered without missing a beat, "Yeah, slow horses."

Where did Rodney Fertel get a taste for these high jinks? Perhaps in the neighborhood where he grew up, South Rampart Street.

He was born in 1921, into a claustrophobic Orthodox Jewish mercantile enclave that was also the center of a whirlwind destined to change world culture. Storyville—the official red-light district where jazz was born—was three blocks away from the Fertel Loan Office, whose motto resonates today: "A Friend in Need Is a Friend Indeed." Rampart Street became the home of jazz after the navy shut Storyville down, unhappy that sailors bound for the Great War detrained on Basin Street opposite Lulu White's Mahogany Hall, so named for the color of the Creole girls there.

On Rampart, just a couple blocks from the Fertels, a kid named Louis Armstrong would walk along singing for coins in his first quartet, his singing so good that a friend dragged Jelly Roll Morton across Canal from Storyville to hear it.

At the corner of Perdido and South Rampart—two

blocks up from the Fertels—the tradition's first greats, Buddy Bolden, Jelly Roll Morton, Kid Ory, "King" Oliver, and Armstrong himself, played the Eagle Saloon, named for the one-time Eagle Loan Office it replaced. Perdido was named during the Spanish colonial period, perhaps because it was low and was often "lost" when it rained. Sure enough, Perdido and Rampart, three blocks from the Superdome, saw water in Katrina's wake.

It was one door off that corner where a younger Louis purchased his first cornet from Jake Fink, my great-aunt Nettie's father-in-law. At that corner, too, out front, Louis, a boy of eleven, was seized by police for firing a sidearm to celebrate New Year's Eve, a local custom that survives to this day. Some believe that was just his story, that in fact he was shooting at some rival. It was a violent world. Trudged off to the Colored Waifs' Home for Boys, he there got his first serious instruction in the cornet. American and world culture would never be the same. Near that corner lay the first home of Zulu, the black Mardi Gras krewe of which Louis Armstrong would one day proudly be king.

Louis Armstrong's spirit, like my father's, haunts South Rampart Street. Born into a depraved and sordid world of hookers and gamblers and pimps, of violence and abuse and racism, Louis believed he could transform the world through music and through laughter. "To hear Louis tell it, or sing it, or blow it," one biographer, Laurence Bergreen, comments, "no one else had ever enjoyed as privileged an existence as his New Orleans boyhood." The Gorilla Man's ready laugh still echoes in my ear.

Not much of the Rampart Street heritage remains to be saved, but that's not Katrina's fault. Much of it was lost long ago to urban planning and to decay.

⁂

When I made my first trip back, New Orleans was unspeakably lonely. The devastation goes on and on, block after block in Lakeview (where I grew up) and Mid-City (where my mother lived) and Lower Bywater and the Ninth Ward—areas once shimmering with funky life and with memories, now just gray and lifeless and forlorn. Lost.

There were dump trucks everywhere, men with masks directing traffic, huge dumping areas piling ever higher, flooded cars everywhere, one surprise detour after another, blocks and blocks boarded up. Everywhere you go you look for the high-water line, sometimes inches from the ground, sometimes feet, sometimes over your head. In Audubon Park, which backs up to my backyard, there are huge holes in the sky where live oaks and water oaks once stood. It's overwhelming and sad.

⁂

In the midst of all of this, we must remember to pay tribute to the canny ingenuousness of Louis Armstrong and the Gorilla Man expressed through laughter and through music. We must remember the birthplace of jazz. We must reach out to the musicians who, now in the Katrina diaspora, live in Austin and New York, Baton Rouge and Houston. We must continue to value the eccentric residents—and those who appreciate their antics. Without those memories and those people, New Orleans, despite all the president's goodwill and federal money or because of it, is in danger of being rebuilt as a soulless Disney World or Las Vegas rather than the vibrant culture that we know and love.

Louis Armstrong was found on *lost* street. Let's pray the New Orleans we've lost is next.

Orpheus

CHRISTOPHER RICE

Today is Lundi Gras, the day before Fat Tuesday. After almost a full week of nightly parades and beer busts, a few brave souls have decided to go in to work. The city is still filled with tourists and the kids are free from school for the rest of the week.

I get out of bed early, a challenge since the Krewe of Bacchus rolled through my neighborhood the night before and I have a fondness for the plastic drink cups their riders toss from their enormous multicolored floats. (So many of the other Mardi Gras parades throw cups that are one solid, gaudy color—bright red or bright green—but Bacchus cups are silvery and translucent, which highlights their illustration of the God of Wine lifting a goblet to his mouth.) As a float captain (one of the youngest) for the Krewe of Orpheus, I will spend the next eight hours shepherding twenty riders, most of them first-timers from out of town, through the strange rituals that lead up to the start of a Mardi Gras parade.

The floats are lined up outside the Morial Convention Center when I arrive. Orpheus is a night parade, and in the morning sunlight its elaborate double-decker floats are almost blinding, their color schemes designed for nighttime magic combining pinks and oranges, garish in the daylight. Massive blossoms fashioned of papier-mâché line the sides of every float. Unlike many other Mardi Gras parades, which slap a large set piece of some kind onto the front of a double-decker float—the head of Louis Armstrong or the face of Poseidon—and simply paint the rest, Orpheus harkens back to the classic and wildly elaborate designs of early Mardi Gras. It is the brainchild of famed musician Harry Connick, Jr.

While the float designs may be classic, the rest of the organization is Mardi Gras for the new millennium. Membership is open to any man or woman willing to pay the $750 membership fee. Each year, several A-list celebrities join the procession as "celebrity monarchs" and the parade is followed by a rock-concert-style ball called the Orpheuscapade.

Parade day is divided into loading up and lining up. The parade itself is referred to as "the ride." For hours, float riders scramble desperately to load their floats with enough "throws" to last them for the duration. Experienced riders spend every last minute until the parade starts hammering nails into the surfaces around them to hold the most coveted of their throws, big necklaces. Small mountains of cardboard boxes are filled with plastic cups bearing the Orpheus logo. Plastic bags of metallic beads and plastic pearls are overstuffed to the splitting point. Ice chests. Trays of sandwiches. Giant speakers, only one of which is likely to remain operational for the duration of the ride. It all must fit somehow. There is, every year, that moment when I just *know* that we simply are not going to be able to fit it all on.

We do it, though, because we must meet the biggest challenge of being a member of a "super-krewe," the term for the enormous parades dominating the city streets the weekend before Fat Tuesday. Every year we receive letters from the organization asking us to be generous with our throws; just like summer festival films, Mardi Gras parades are often harshly judged by the quality and quantity of the shiny gifts riders dole out to their screaming audiences. And every year I purchase more throws than can possibly be crammed onboard our float, and gladly. In Mardi Gras life, nothing, absolutely nothing, is worse than running out of beads before the parade passes the finish line. Only a jousted knight has known such impotence. So this year, as every year, instead of standing, my riders will spend the hours in transit from the Convention Center to our starting point in Uptown New Orleans, sitting atop a five-foot pile of Carnival loot.

Lineup begins with a deceptive burst of excitement, the sudden revving of tractor engines as the floats slowly peel away from the Convention Center. The NOPD has stopped traffic to allow us to pass, and drivers step out of stalled cars on the Mississippi River Bridge to wave at us as we pass beneath them. Then the ride settles into a lumbering trip up Tchoupitoulas Street. Children pour out of tiny shotgun houses, pleading for a string of long white pearls, but local law prohibits us from throwing anything off the float until we have reached our starting point. By now first-timers are wondering just what they have gotten themselves into. Their legs are cramped. The bathroom is a bucket inside a tiny room in the center of the float, but riders have driven nails through its walls; if we hit a bump, the bathroom becomes an Iron Maiden. I have sent them an egregiously long letter explaining the tedious process leading up to the orgiastic burst of pleasure awaiting them as the ride begins. Of course, not one of them has actually read it. An editor of mine from New York sits rigidly atop his pile of beads, glaring into a volume of *Remembrance of Things Past*. He would appear almost studious if he weren't dressed entirely in gold lamé like the rest of us. His nod to Proust strikes the few locals on board as somehow irreverent, conveying an outsider's suspicion of what lies ahead.

Just when the biting wind off the nearby river becomes too much to bear, the fuel truck appears, passing from tractor pull to tractor pull, filling each gas-powered generator and setting each float's automated strings of lights ablaze. Sound systems begin belching modern hip-hop or time-honored Mardi Gras classics such as "They All Axed for You." Then, finally, there are the first forward lurches of movement and riders who have been anxiously circling the parked float scurry back on board, taking care to fasten their safety harnesses as soon as they are in place, something I have reminded them to do about six hundred times since our float left the Convention Center.

Of course, I have staked out the best spot on the float for myself; second position in the forward section of the float, on the coveted "sidewalk side," so as we approach our starting point in a series of false starts and jerking stops, I can see the sea of people awaiting our arrival just outside Tipitina's Bar and Grill. Ahead of us, a float makes the final turn and suddenly its decks erupt with spiraling plastic beads and sleeves of plastic cups that separate from one another in midair. Every year I wish I had a camera to capture the expression on the faces of my riders as we make this turn. But I can see the evidence of their enthusiasm; the handfuls of plastic beads they sling high into the air over the sea of grasping hands.

Then there is the moment when our float pulls to a stop in front of my mother's house on St. Charles Avenue. Here, the four hundred guests who have been at my family's open house for the entire weekend cover the sidewalk and cling to the wrought-iron front fence. Within seconds, they are raising their arms to shield their faces as bags of white plastic pearls tear open on the spokes of the front fence and smash on the pavement and their contents are yanked away by children grappling with one another for the prizes. (One year, we broke a front window of the house.) This deluge, a cause for litigation in other cities, lasts for about three minutes, thanks to a few twenties we slipped our tractor driver before the parade started. By the time we are done, most of our friends, who were convinced we wouldn't see them, are limping back toward the house, their arms full of trash-turned-treasure, angry red welts rising on their foreheads.

Orpheus ends right back where it started, at the Convention Center. In its absence, however, a magical transformation has turned two enormous halls into the Orpheuscapade. As our float idles outside an open cargo door in the side of the Convention Center, new riders think we're about to enter an empty warehouse. Instead, our float rounds another corner, where it is greeted by a roar rarely heard outside of a football stadium. Our float snakes through a sea of white tablecloths, men in tuxedos and ladies in sequined evening dresses balancing precariously atop folding chairs. Now that we're inside, we can finally hear the music of the marching bands that have been in front of and behind us throughout the ride. We pass the VIP seating area and receive the joyful welcome of Orpheus Captain Sonny Borey. We have arrived.

In his *Six Elements of Drama,* Aristotle wrote that a spectacle should exist not merely for the sake of spectacle but should also contribute to the plot. Tonight's spectacle has contributed directly to the action, the ongoing drama of a great city steeped in the arts essential to enjoying the theater of life. It has affirmed our collective belief that revelry is the spiritual right of each man and woman, to be displayed and doled out in great plastic handfuls to anyone willing to stake out a position on the sidewalk, not hidden behind the veils of old-world traditions. Access is granted to all, not on the basis of privilege alone. To the uninitiated, Mardi Gras might seem an act of reckless debauchery. To those who have experienced it and understand it, Mardi Gras is an act of fearless generosity.

Daughters . . .

New Orleans

Alleys secreting pirate plots,
Mystery of moss-robed oaks.
Serene smiles of old ample houses,
Startle of skyscrapers mocking a
sultry sky.
Jazz suffusion.

Swamps sulking to be free
       beneath your streets,
River beating at your banks
      to beat you out,
Somehow some native stuff
Out of which you are made has
baffled them.
You know them better than they
know you.
Eternal flirt of a city,
Creole witch-eyed survivor
of fire and oil famine,
Masking your courage with Mardi Gras.
Gaiety and guts.

—BARBARA BOGGS SIGMUND

The Secret Ingredient

ELLA BRENNAN

The secret ingredient in that treasured recipe called New Orleans is the people who live here—the natives who simply can't stand to be anywhere else for very long and those who came here by choice and stayed forever because they couldn't stand to be anyplace else for very long, and our friends who keep coming back because they get it. They understand why we can't stand to be anyplace else for very long.

New Orleans is blessed. We are an extraordinary community of people who are, for the most part, nonconformists. We have a different attitude about the way we live. Unlike most Americans, for instance, we do not spend a lot of time worrying about what others think of us.

In a lot of other places, even in other parts of the South, people frequently strike me as sugarcoated cookies, all the same color of vanilla with the same number of sugar beads on top, all turned out by a bored chef with a cookie cutter. It's the corporate mold, I guess. It's a big deal out there in the rest of America, being a corporate bigwig. They talk a lot about how much money they make and the tax breaks they need to make them richer, and, for God's sake, golf. Give me a break! Those corporate chiefs out there in the rest of the world wouldn't be caught dead boogeying in the streets with the Mardi Gras Indians. They all buy the same Brooks Brothers shirts and loafers and gray flannel suits and old-school-type ties, apparently worried that they might actually be noticed in a crowd.

New Orleans counterparts actually court the recognition of the crowd. Where else in America would the CEO of a major corporation give his last dollar for the chance to prance around in a crown and pink tights on Fat Tuesday, to ascend a throne and wave a scepter about grandly to a crowd screaming, "Hail, Rex"?

The wives of corporate America wear the same little white tennis skirts and tennis bracelets and carry the same little Vuitton purses when they are on their way to the right country clubs, where they talk a lot about what the right people are doing and the right friends for their children over their little plates of lettuce. They don't care much about what they eat as long as it doesn't have any fat or sugar or taste in it to make them gain an ounce.

New Orleans women dress to be noticed, wearing interesting clothes, which are rarely the *dernier cri* but are frequently memorable. A close, longtime friend had a mild form of schizophrenia. Intelligent and articulate and charming, she also was beautiful and much admired for her flair with clothes, which she wore like a model. Occasionally, she would forget to take her pills, however, and then she was really unforgettable. One day at Commander's Palace, a mutual friend, Pokey McIlhenney of the Tabasco McIlhenneys, called me on the phone and said, "Have you looked outside?" I had not and she said, "Go to the window, now!" Our friend was walking up to the door of Commander's in full runway stride in nothing but her panties and bra, waving to friends getting out of their cars. She had the body and was cutting quite the figure. No one condemned her or was scandalized by the incident. It was the stuff New Orleans legends are made of; we understood she had broken out of the mold to be her other self.

Unlike her, most New Orleans women, of course, always are in search of the right diet because they love food and delight in the preparation of it and the ceremonial presentation of it. And they'd give up the fashion plate for the dinner plate and the joys *à table* any old day.

New Orleanians are not emulators. They are individuals—sometimes distant, sometimes engaging, sometimes rugged or intellectual, and other times, frankly, just absurdly eccentric, but almost always original.

There are, of course, those among us who feel more secure with the protective coloring of their instantly recognizable status symbols and more comfortable in their cliques. In New Orleans, however, most of us break out of the mold in some way every day and those who do not are in the minority.

We live pretty much the way we want to live and we

don't really care whether you approve of how we live or not. At the same time, we accept that our individual lifestyles might not be either satisfying or possible for others and we are tolerant of all the others who choose or are forced by circumstances to live or behave in different ways.

There are many layers to this *dobèrge* of a city. The layers are separate and distinct and the people who are the ingredients of each layer have their own special quirks, their unique ways of speaking, their celebratory customs, and their foods. Each layer is worthy of exploring. But when you cut the cake on special occasions and get a slice of each layer all at the same time, well, the taste is nothing short of sensational. The icing on the cake, the tie that binds, is our love of our life together and our city.

We are responsible people. We take care of each other because, and I truly believe this, we genuinely love each other, regardless of which layer of the cake is ours.

And we are hospitable to one another and to outsiders. Because we are geographically isolated from the rest of the country, outsiders are our diversion. We take them to our hearts and into our homes and we nurture them and we become their friends for life and we love them, as long as they don't abuse our hospitality. Even then, we tend to be a forgiving sort if they have an interesting story to tell.

The great storytellers, those who have come to New Orleans and fallen in love with her and write about her and keep coming back to her, pick up on this and in the end they, too, become a part of the fabric of life here.

When I was a very young girl, my older brother Owen Edward Brennan was my idol. And I hung on his coattails. He was kind and tolerated me as his ever constant shadow. After World War II, he operated the Absinthe House at the corner of Bienville and Bourbon Streets. It was the chic place to be in those days and well-known New Orleanians, such as Count Arnaud, the eccentric Frenchman who started one of the best of the city's old-line restaurants, were regular patrons. One night Arnaud and Owen were talking about food and restaurants, and Arnaud declared that it would "be totally impossible for an Irishman like you to run a successful restaurant." Owen took that as a dare, a challenge to his heritage. He accepted the challenge and shortly thereafter our family, all of us, found ourselves squarely in the middle of the restaurant business, helping Owen prove to Arnaud that an Irishman could give a Frenchman a run for his money any old day. Owen convinced my father, Owen Patrick, to retire and join him in the challenge. We opened the Vieux Carré restaurant right across the street from Owen's Absinthe House, and that was the beginning of what we call Brennan's Family of Restaurants. It was Owen's job to get the customers, and he was the best Music Man ever to grace God's earth. It was ours to make sure they came back again and again.

After hours, Owen would walk down Bourbon

Street nine blocks to Café Lafitte, with me trailing along after him. During that nightly stroll, we would stop and speak to maybe a hundred people, all of them Owen's friends, as we made our way to our late-night destination. Café Lafitte attracted all of the great talents in town. Tennessee Williams could be found there every night he was in town. You might run into the lead dancer for the Ballets Russes or a film star or actors in a hit play or the fabulous Mexican sculptor Enrique Alferez or politicians such as Hubert Humphrey and Eugene McCarthy or local politicos such as Earl Long or Chep Morrison or famous authors and syndicated journalists such as Robert Rouark. Bob Rouark had this electrifying charisma, and I am not ashamed to say I fell head over heels in love with him the first time I met him at Café Lafitte. He became a mentor for me, as did others. I became absolutely enamoured with café society and its celebrity cast. I did not go to college. I was in the business immediately after high school. But the people I met at Café Lafitte and at the Vieux Carré and the Absinthe House were the best possible education anyone could have. Bob Rouark taught me everything—which magazines and newspapers to read, which books to read, where to travel and why, how to get over my shyness and have a conversation. Lucius Beebe, who loves trains and drinks and writes about both a lot, used to send me books he wanted me to read. They all gave me advice for living. They all became friends for life.

One day Rouark called me from Washington to ask

if I had read the latest *Time* magazine. I said yes, of course, as I was always doing my homework. "Did you notice anything special?" he asked. "No, just the news." He told me to look at it carefully and then call him back and tell him what I saw. I combed that thing and still could not for the life of me figure out what he was trying to tell me. So I called him back and said, "I give up." He asked me, "What is the date on your copy?" I told him and he said, "You really are behind the times down there on the bayous." He told me to go out to the newsstand and get the *current* issue of *Time*. When I asked the news dealer for the magazine with the right date, he said, "Well, we won't get that for a couple more days."

I was beside myself, of course, and wrung my hands until I finally got the right magazine, and there he was, my friend, on the cover.

I adored them all and, of course, I took their advice on life. I traveled and, invariably, I would meet one of them and, invariably, it was good for business because they loved New Orleans too. I ran into Jim Beard and Art Buchwald on the town in Paris and Jim began to tell Buchwald about New Orleans and the great food at Brennan's. The next thing I knew a column by Buchwald on the ten best restaurants in the world appeared in *The Herald Tribune* and, guess what, he had listed Brennan's as number one.

After those marvelous, heady days and nights, I could never settle for anything less. I always wanted to know who was new or who was doing something new and interesting in town and to meet them and have them at the restaurant—at Brennan's or later Commander's— for dinner and listen to their stories in the company of friends.

That's how I have operated Commander's Palace, as if throwing an ongoing dinner party for my friends, providing the same kind of hospitality for our patrons that I would provide in my own home, making sure the guests are welcomed properly, that they are comfortable, that the service is perfect—never obtrusive or interrupting, because to me, the conversation over dinner is what the party is about, along with the food, of course. The food should not be overly complicated, however, just fresh and good, the kind of food that makes you happy.

Sometimes New Orleans can make you so sad, though. Our greatest asset, our ability to forget our cares and enjoy life, is also our failing. Like other cities, New Orleans has failed to overhaul its public education system, failed to come to grips with the poverty that invariably is the result of inferior education. And we frequently fail to throw out the bums in politics until after they've done a lot of damage.

At least we have a sense of humor about our foibles, however.

One of my best friends from my salad days was David Brinkley. He came to New Orleans frequently and every time he was in town we would have dinner, usually with other friends. On one of his last visits, he called me up and said, let's have dinner, but just the two of us. Let's just sit down together and talk about New Orleans.

Well, we did, and I began to explain to him how depressed I was about the future of the city because City Hall was a mess and we were not doing anything about the public schools and unemployment and drugs and crime. My tale of woe went on for an hour or so, I guess. Then we changed the subject to more pleasant topics.

The next day, however, he called me and said, "Ella, I am worried about you. You seem too depressed. The state of the city is making you too sad." I acknowledged that he was right, that I was frustrated by my inability to make good things happen and worried sick that people would stop coming.

"Let me explain something, Ella. Have you been to Italy?" he asked.

"Of course. I adore Italy and go back as often as I can. I love the food. I love the people. I love the architecture, everything about it."

Then he said, "Did you notice that everything is falling apart?"

I had to admit that I had not.

"Will you stop going to Italy because they can't get the trains to run on time?"

"You're right, I'll keep going to Italy forever . . . but in New Orleans, David, we say 'Idaly.' "

Funkytown, or How New Orleans Made Me a Birdwatcher

POPPY Z. BRITE

I never much liked birds. Something about their beady eyes annoyed me, and my now-husband, then-hippie-boyfriend traumatized me years ago by causing me to appear in an embarrassing guerrilla street theater production of Aristophanes' *The Birds*. Occasionally, when I was in a really foul mood, I'd rap on the window and scare away any I saw perching outside.

I've always liked Audubon Park, though, and when I moved Uptown in 1995, its proximity was one of my favorite aspects of my new neighborhood. I grew up out East, back when there was oil money there (not that we had any); I had my sixth birthday party in Joe Brown Park and now I felt better with another big expanse of greenery nearby. At some point I began going to Audubon several times a week and walking around the 1.75-mile track in an attempt to get some exercise. It wasn't much, but in a writer's life, going downstairs to get a Diet Coke from the fridge qualifies as exercise; a good bar crawl is our version of a marathon. For the first time in years, I was actually attempting to do something healthy.

As writers often do when they set out to improve their lives, I got distracted. What distracted me? Well, it was the birds.

Here I must digress to tell you about a different animal altogether, a cat we got a couple of years before I started taking these walks. William is a pure white oriental shorthair. He's beautiful, but also faintly ridiculous in his combination of gawkiness and grace. Something about his snowy coloration, long limbs, and pointed face reminded us of the white egrets we'd seen on our drives through south Louisiana. William is sweet-natured, but hates to be picked up; when you try, he flails about and pumps his elbows and does a very credible version of that popular '60s dance the Funky Chicken. We started calling him the Funky Egret, which also evolved into my Internet handle.

So my fondness for William disposed me to like egrets, even if I didn't care for most other birds. And in Audubon Park, on Ochsner Island in the middle of the lagoon, is possibly the most extensive egret nesting area to be found in the heart of any major American city. They may range far and wide, but these are urban egrets, as I acknowledged in one of the pieces of bird doggerel that began to corrode my mind eventually:

> *I caught a fish*
> *On Rocheblave*

The Urban Egret
Burma-Shave

But that was much later. Early on, I just slowed down in my walks now and then, and sometimes even sat at the edge of the lagoon to watch the avian dramas unfolding across the water. I quickly learned to identify the different species: the big ones with yellow bills and black legs were great egrets; the little delicate ones with ebony bills and legs and bright yellow "shoes" were snowy egrets; the stocky, pompous-looking ones were cattle egrets. When I realized there were other kinds of birds on the island too—not flitty little songbirds, which I still didn't care about, but other large, charismatic waders—I succumbed to temptation and bought a book. I learned that the dirty-white chicken-size birds with ridiculously long curved bills were white ibises, and I began to see them as the tricksters of the rookery, the badly behaved cousins who snarfed up all the good fishing spots and nested in the highest branches so they could crap on everybody else. I identified the slender blue-gray ones with bright blue bills as little blue herons and the pretty pied ones as tricolor herons, also known as Louisiana herons. I learned that the colloquial name for the crow-size green heron is "shitpoke," and that these cranky little birds steal stale bread from the ducks and scatter it on the water's surface to attract fish. One day I talked to a pair of hungry-looking Cajuns from Eunice and learned what all the various birds tasted like; long before Bobby Hebert replaced my beloved Buddy D on the radio, I learned that the little black paddlers I knew as coots are called *poules d'eau* in Cajun country, and that Catholics are allowed to eat them on Lenten Fridays, since they are considered several evolutionary levels below fish.

When all the birds on the island began nesting in late spring, I was lost. I bought a pair of binoculars, the first I'd ever owned, and came to the park every day until little fuzzy heads began to poke above the edges of nests. The baby egrets resembled nothing so much as Muppets; true to form, the baby ibises soon grew as large as their parents, and fed by thrusting their heads, necks, and shoulders down their parents' throats as if trying to consume their very stomach contents. Like any interesting scene in New Orleans, the rookery was noisy and smelly and full of strife; I had previously thought cats were the great drama queens of the animal kingdom, but birds have them beat all to hell.

Since that spring several years ago, I've become an avid birder, interested in all species, not just waders. I've amassed a life list. I subscribe to bird newsletters on the Internet. I've gone to the other side of the world—the tropical rainforests of northern Australia—to see one of the world's rarest and weirdest birds, the flightless, six-foot-tall southern cassowary. As I have said, I write bird doggerel—never poetry, I won't dignify it with the title, but little things like this:

I only catch the freshest fish
Instead of eating trash and poo
Thank God I am a pelican
And not a crappy gull like you.

I've never forgotten, though, that my interest in birds had its genesis in the heart of New Orleans. This makes perfect sense to me; almost everything that interests me has its origins in New Orleans, or at least some connection to the city. The rookery on Ochsner Island is just another way in which the city demonstrates that, in addition to all the interesting things outsiders expect of us, we are full of secret treasures, too.

Home Is Still New Orleans

Patty Friedmann

It is my nature to find irony everywhere, and when I was trapped in New Orleans for a week after Hurricane Katrina hit, I was amused despite the horror, thinking about what I had written for the *Smith Alumnae Quarterly* a month before. I was supposed to address how I felt about my home. My opening paragraph was to read:

When a tropical storm starts building toward hurricane strength in the Gulf of Mexico, I begin to imagine that people all over the place think about me, worry about me. "The storm is located 294 miles southeast of New Orleans," the meteorologist will say, and quite a number of people know only one person in New Orleans, me. Including high school mates. The city isn't just my birthplace; it's my identity. I squat here furiously, as if someone else will become the person in New Orleans if I go away for more than a few days. I never evacuate during hurricanes.

As an individual, but probably more as a writer, I don't like to be away from New Orleans. Last year when

Hurricane Ivan was heading toward New Orleans I was in Houston. When the airport closed, I rented a car and drove back, my plucky little Taurus the only vehicle zipping east while a traffic jam was inching west on the other side of the interstate. New Orleans always has been a mother to me. Vain, disheveled, and not very responsible, but the only mother I've ever known.

A critic once said that the reason Southern writers are particularly skewed is that they never leave home. He explained that staying in one place allows a writer to watch the generations go by. He was thinking of small towns, and oddly, even before the flood, New Orleans always was a small town, a water-locked trap where absolutely everyone was a gossipy old woman. What has paralyzed and mesmerized me forever are this small town's very urban traits, which are playing so poorly in the national media: the squalor and lawlessness and strange beauty. These are the reasons I've never been able to leave.

My departure was arduous and inevitable, by rowboat and a waist-deep wade through filth and truck rides all over Louisiana and finally a pickup by my son, who came from Houston to get me in Baton Rouge, his car loaded with seventeen one-gallon cans of gasoline. I never cried until we crossed the Texas state line and I saw that big ol' lit-up star and I knew I was leaving behind my greatest love, who perhaps would be taken off life support by the federal government. That's when I burst into tears.

I've been asked whether I'm having trouble with my identity as a New Orleanian now that I've been taken out of place. So far, it's just the opposite. As I write, the hurricane is still front-page news, and wherever I go in Houston, all I have to do is say, "I'm from New Orleans," and people are kind and gentle and generous. New Orleans is suddenly a national treasure. I thought my novel *Side Effects* would have to be abandoned because it is about a city that doesn't exist. It doesn't matter to my publisher. To everyone who doesn't live there, New Orleans is an imaginary place. To me, everywhere else feels the same. I'm like Ciana, one of the characters in the book. This is how I expect to go back to New Orleans:

Every trip Ciana ever has taken ends exactly the same way. She descends at the Carrollton exit, and where she has been is relegated to memory, to perspective stored deep. Carrollton Avenue is that way, dilapidated and out of place in America, and it makes her find it hard to believe she just has been somewhere else. If she has come from an international flight arriving at the airport, if she has come from Baton Rouge; it always has been the same. Ciana figures this is probably why no one ever moves away from New Orleans; natives find everywhere else impossible to believe. This stretch of Carrollton works like Versed, inducing retrograde amnesia. Tonight she has forgotten whatever has happened to her in the past three days.

I'm going back. And I'm going to forget.

The Channel, New Orleans

MARY HELEN LAGASSE

The best days are the first to flee . . .
VIRGIL

These recollections are a paean to the
neighborhood of my youth.

The Irish Channel I knew and loved was bounded by Magazine Street and the Mississippi River, by Washington Avenue and Race Street. It was a true melting pot of cultures and of people.

One story of how the Channel got its name is that seamen negotiating the river on foggy nights watched for the lights kept burning in the Irish pubs—one saloon after the other guiding them safely along the sinuous course of the river. The sailors began to call that area the "Irish Channel," and the name stuck.

In the 1850s, when Irish immigrants crossed Federal Road, passed the cotton presses and foundries that bordered the river, and settled in what came to be known as the Irish Channel, the area was predominantly German. Of the two magnificent churches "built right around the corner from one another," the first, St. Mary's Assumption, was built by the Germans for the German community; the second, St. Alphonsus, was built by the Irish for Irish parishioners.

My friend Laurie and I were three years old when my family moved to the Channel in the early fifties. On windy days we'd sit on the front steps and watch the domed bell tower of St. Mary's scraping the clouds; nights we'd go to bed listening to the chiming of the tower bells and the cries of nighthawks that darted from the eaves to feed on insects caught on the wing. We'd drowse to the hoots of tugboats on the Mississippi, to the sounds of freight trains linking like rusting behemoths along the tracks that lined the wharves a few blocks away. To the north of us was the Garden District; to the south were the riverfront Negro shanties, and all about were shotgun singles, gingerbread doubles, camelback duplexes, corner groceries, and across the street the hundred-twenty-five-block St. Thomas Housing Project—like the Channel, a city unto itself.

To look at our house from across the street, and to get an even closer look and see the name Hernandez on the mailbox in little gold letters my father bought in a packet at Clark & Roescher's, was to see it no different than any of the other houses. What made our house different from my friend Laurie's and everyone else's in the neighborhood was everything that went on inside it—

the everyday things that were governed by my grandmother's *mexicanidad*.

You no sooner walked in than you saw her El Popo Cigars calendar. Even then it was out of date by a couple of years. But she didn't keep it to reckon time; she kept it for the picture of the two volcanoes and the legendary figures with the unpronounceable names—Popocatepetl, which means "Smoking Mountain," and Iztaccihuatl, which means "White Lady." The legend is an Aztec version of "Sleeping Beauty." Not that my grandmother favored romantic legends or rituals, but being Mexican she was fond of most anything Mexican, and those volcanoes pictured in the calendar were sacred mountains nestled in the Valley of Mexico—turf that my grandmother, sleeping year in, year out in the second bedroom of a shotgun house in the heart of the Channel, traversed in her dreams.

Then there were the aromas: *achiote, cilantro, comino, hierba buena, perejil*—tangy, aromatic seeds and fragrant herbs that my grandmother found at the French Market and used in the *guisos* whose scents permeated the house with a bouquet like no other in the neighborhood.

When Laurie and I were old enough to cross the streets unattended, we'd walk the few blocks to Magazine Street—a wonderland of Fisher's Department Store, DeRouen Drugs, Earl's Seafood Restaurant, Baehr's Bakery, Behrman's Dry Goods, Ellzey's Grocery, Hill's Supermarket, Woolworth's Five & Dime, Corona's Bar, the Happy Hour Theater, Young's Antiques, the Magazine Street Market (where your mama bought "fresh hens" on Saturday mornings), Curley's Sweet Shop, and Lizzie's Laundry! We'd run into Laurie's grandparents' laundry shop, scoot under the big drop-leaf panel of the chest-high counter, and beg for the nickels to buy the hard-frozen paper-coned ice cream sold at the Best Ice Cream Parlor, two doors down.

I loved the Guggenheimers almost as much as I loved my own grandmother: Grandpa Eli with his thatch of gray hair, his skin the color of autumn leaves, and his button-down suspenders that reminded me of inverted wishbones; Grandma Lizzie with her plump, downy cheeks, her Irish button nose, and her hairnets flimsy as spiderwebs. I think of the sign that hung from the wrought-iron arm in front of their laundry shop,

Lizzie the Launderer
—SHIRTS EXPERTLY DONE—
—HATS BLOCKED—

and remember the old couple steaming and pressing with those big metal pressers. Lizzie Guggenheimer, a buxom woman, pranced about in slippered feet, toe first, like a dancer; Grandpa Eli, an unlit pipe clenched between his teeth, sat in his chair behind the counter, his good ear pressed to the Emerson radio that *whee-ohhed* whenever he turned the dials in search of transatlantic news. They lived in the two rooms in the back, separated from the shop by a stiffly starched curtain that failed to hold in the aromas of Lizzie's cooking so that, invariably, the shop smelled as much of veal chops smothered in onions (Grandpa Eli's favorite) as it did starches and soaps and cleaning fluids.

That long-ago day when I entered the laundry shop for the first time, I was fascinated by the old War Bonds poster that sighed with the slightest shift of air and cast the shop with a sadness that tinged the bright blue walls and shiny linoleum-covered counters. Yellowed and tattered, the poster was still on the wall of the shop when Grandpa Eli died of a stroke and Grandma Lizzie died of congestive heart failure two years after him; and the Lizzie the Launderer sign stayed out front, dangling from a single hook, until the place was reopened as the electronics repair shop it is today.

Our Slow Curve

LEAH CHASE

In baseball you have fastballs and sliders and, then, there are the low, slow curves. Those slow curves come at you low down and they'll hit you in the knees, hard, making you go down and out if you don't hit them first. The low, slow curve is hard to hit, but if you do hit it, that ball is out of the park.

Katrina is our slow curve.

We have got to hit it now.

I believe we will.

And I believe the salvation of New Orleans will be, as it ever has been, its people. We all know, all of us know, that this country cannot afford to lose New Orleans. It's like no other place in the world because we care for one another. Losing New Orleans would be worse than losing New York . . . and mind you, I love New York, love visiting that Big Apple, there are so many sights to see . . . but in New York you can lose one another in the hustle and bustle. And one side of the city may never see the other side. And I don't mean to pick on New York or other cities that have been so kind to the people of New Orleans in our time of tragedy. It's just that in most other places on a day-to-day basis, people are so preoccupied with themselves, their work or lack of it, their private lives, they just don't see each other.

We're not like that in New Orleans.

Walking down the street, we smile at one another and say something nice, at least "Hello" or "Good to see you," or as the fellows like to say, walking up to one another with a grin and slapping hand to hand, "Where y'at." We notice each other. We care about each other. We take time with each other.

People have been talking a lot on TV about how bad the projects are in New Orleans, and it's true, a lot of poor people live in the projects, just barely making it, and there is a lot of drug trafficking in them. But people in these old projects, such as the Lafitte Project on Orleans across from Dooky Chase, help each other. The junkies who live there, for instance, help the old people, the children, too.

We had an old aunt who was the first resident of the Lafitte Project when it opened in the late '30s about the same time as Dooky's. She could have moved but it had been her home too long. It was her neighborhood and people took care of her there and made sure she was not lonely. Before she died in 1992, she fell down and hurt herself. Some of those same people picked her up, took her up to her apartment, and laid her down and called the doctor to come look at her. They never touched a thing in her apartment. They picked her up and got medical help and they got things for her to eat.

There were a lot of little Robin Hoods, some of them project junkies, I'm sure, running around after Katrina, and for the first time in the sixty-seven years Dooky Chase has been operating, we were looted. But I understand. The restaurant was closed. We were gone. There was food in the restaurant and those people in the project needed to be fed. It would be mean-spirited for me to be mad at them. The food would have spoiled and the old people in the project would have starved without them.

In New Orleans we have a sense of community. New Orleanians generally are very unselfish, Samaritans, and will always give you something if you are without.

Dooky Chase is in a black neighborhood but people from all over the city, white and black and every color in between, come to talk about their music or their politics, or just to see each other and eat *gumbo z'herbes,* fried chicken, collard greens, rice and gravy, and bread pudding, all our comfort food. This has been going on since 1939, when Dooky and I first opened our doors. And true New Orleanians feel good together under the same roof, comfortable in their own skin.

When the Zulu Ball rolls around, there's a rainbow crowd—Creoles from all over the city, gays from the Marigny, artists and writers and journalists and Italians from the Quarter, doctors and lawyers and professors from Lakeview and old Metairie, and the Bigwigs from Uptown, and politicians, and, of course, our out-of-town guests of every stripe, too. They all like to go and have fun together and they're not afraid to rub shoulders so they do have fun, a lot of fun, and our sense of fun together will be part of our salvation too.

We may live apart but we go out every day and meet each other. We know each other. We live separately for the most part in our own neighborhoods, the ones we grew up in, and we love our neighborhoods and cling to them. Unlike most cities, New Orleans is fortunate to have had, always, so many stable neighborhoods, such as the Seventh Ward, Treme, and the Esplanade Ridge, and Gentilly, and Bywater and the Lower Ninth Ward and Lakeview and the Garden District and the Vieux Carré . . . and the strength of these neighborhoods will be a part of our salvation too, because the strength of these neighborhoods is their people.

I have been all over and there are no people anywhere like New Orleanians. We're different. We love our city so very much more, we are just nuts about our place . . . for sure, it's the food and the way we enjoy sharing it with each other and the good smells of it cooking . . . for sure, it's the music, and that music, I don't know, it's just always there in the air. It's also having something unique to live in, our pretty little shotgun houses, our pretty camelback houses, and our Creole cottages, which came to us from Africa and France and Spain and through the Islands and were melded into our own style and which all have enough room in them for people to move around and stoops we can sit on and visit with our neighbors and watch out for them. And our old projects, too. They were built at a time when things were built right. These brick buildings are solid and strong and they could be pretty, too, with some renovation and landscaping. We need to find a way to keep them and recycle them in a better way. We might have to live in trailers temporarily until we can make things right, but we have to do everything in our power to keep our city from turning into a permanent "trailer town." The thought of that is frightening to me; I wake up in the middle of the night thinking about those poor people in Florida still living in trailers for so long since their bad storm.

We've been plenty poor in New Orleans but we've always had a space to live in; and no matter how poor we were, we always tried to look good.

As my mamma used to say, "Fix yourself up, look good. We don't want to run around looking like Joe Lapicote." I don't know who Joe Lapicote was, just that he was trashy looking and all the old Creole ladies who raised me used that phrase and I knew it meant we were not to go out of house without fixing ourselves up so that we looked nice. People in New Orleans like to be noticed, it's part of our style, and every one of us, I don't care how poor, has something in their closet to put on and to give us a little shine. I see those children of the project across the street, for example. I see them going out to school every morning. They are clean, they have on clean clothes, their hair is combed and they have it fixed neatly in cornrow braids or other styles, and they have on some bit of bright color. New Orleanians don't go out of the house without fixing up as best they can, and that usually means in a way to catch other people's attention.

We are very conservative in many ways in New Orleans and that, too, will be important in figuring out our salvation.

I have faith that we can have New Orleans like we had it before, as we are stubborn about our beautiful old houses, our neighborhoods, our traditions, our food, our music, living easy. We need to make it better, too, however. It took this disaster to bring home hard to us that 50 percent of New Orleanians are simply unable to fend for themselves.

The New Orleans of the future simply cannot be a city in which 50 percent of the people are unable to fend for themselves.

My parents used to tell us that "if you don't take care of the child, then you will be taking care of the adult forever." And that is what has happened to us. We have failed to educate many of our children, we have failed to give them the tools with which to work, and we have failed to teach them the value of work. And those we failed to take care of as children are those who today are unable to fend for themselves. We are not alone among American cities in this failure. Every major American city has a similar situation, and if they are struck by a disaster too, they will find that huge numbers of their people will be left behind because they cannot fend for themselves.

I believe in God and that things happen for reasons known to God. It's not hard to figure out what our superior being wants, however. I know it's no longer politically correct to say "what He wants," but He wants us to help each other as we have always done, now more than ever before.

God has a way of reshuffling things every now and then.

In the aftermath of Katrina, many black people were evacuated to places such as Utah, where there were hardly any black people. If they find jobs and a new life and don't come back because they have a better life in Utah, that's part of the reshuffling, finding a way and fending for themselves.

And, who knows, maybe plain vanilla old Utah will be better too, with some color in its life for a change.

God has shown us, big time, that we need to fix the things that were wrong, such as the schools, and that we need to get rid of this concept of something for nothing. Even during the Depression, when we didn't have two nickels to rub together, my daddy wouldn't let us take anything. He wanted us to learn to get by in hard times. We need to teach our children the meaning of work, both the value and the pleasure of it. There's been too much of something for nothing in our city and our society generally. And I worry about what the young people will do if a depression comes like we had, because they don't understand what it's like to *really* be without.

Work makes the world go around. I am in my eighties and I cook every day of my life and it gives my life meaning. Even the pope has to eat, after all. But I can't operate my business without waiters and sous chefs and busboys and dishwashers and house cleaners and advertising copywriters and public relations people. I don't have the education and experience, perhaps, to be president, but I can feed the president and he'll be very happy with the food I put on his table.

We must close in on the business of uplifting.

We must make people understand that all work is good work by making all of our people understand that we value what each does for the other.

A good example of what I am talking about came out of a party we had recently to say thanks to the men and women who helped us in our efforts to restore the historic cemeteries of New Orleans, our Cities of the Dead. A man who had helped significantly said, "I can clean bricks without breaking them and my wife can clean bricks without breaking them. If we do this, then it is easier for the bricklayers to come in and make repairs and for the plasterers to come in and plaster over the bricks." He was very proud of what he had done to help restore the cemeteries. Recognizing everyone's accomplishments, not just those of the man at the top, will help us now in rebuilding New Orleans, in fixing the things that are wrong.

And we need to strengthen the things that were right. Instead of spending a lot of time spinning our wheels right now over attracting new industry, we need to fix our broken hospitality and food and entertainment industries and expand them. We don't have time right now to reinvent the wheel. These are the things we do well and they will save us as they have in the past.

God threw us a lowdown slow curve but he does not want us to strike out. He wants us to make it, to hit the ball out of the park. He provides little signposts for us, showing us he is pulling for that hit.

There is in that horrifying jumble of splintered family homes in Lakeview two of these signs, two oases: a park by St. Dominic's, and in that park the statue of the Blessed Mother still stands with arms outstretched; and in that devastated neighborhood, some small groups of houses that had next to no damage, no water. They are symbols of what was and what can be again.

The statue of Jesus in St. Anthony's Garden behind St. Louis Cathedral is still standing, miraculously, his arms raised in forgiveness, when the garden's three-hundred-year-old oak tree was uprooted and blown to pieces, sending branches every which way. The French Quarter and the CBD and the Garden District were up and running again first, there to put their hands down and lift the others up to the good life.

We are ready to help ourselves, too, Mr. Mayor, Mr. Entergy. If you'll just, finally, get the lights turned back on, that ball will be going, going, gone!

Come as You Are

Charmaine Neville

My New Orleans is all about us, her people. We move it and shake it a little bit more down here, you know, and a lot better . . . and our faith is stronger, regardless of whether we are Catholic or Baptist or Jewish or Muslim or Episcopalian or whatever . . . and we are more hospitable—we just plain have better manners than most people in other places.

When I was growing up, it didn't matter if I passed old Miss Mattie sitting on her stoop seventeen times a day, each time I passed by her I had to say, "Hello, Miss Mattie, how are you doing, Miss Mattie, you feeling okay, Miss Mattie?" That's the way we were brought up, to be polite and kind to one another, and so it just comes naturally for us to be hospitable with outsiders, too.

I love the way we are with each other, so happy to just be together, so laid back and easy. At the root of it all, deep down, all of us love each other, just like brothers and sisters.

It's this feeling that will bring back all of those New Orleanians scattered in distant places like Utah! Utah, can you believe that? And Houston, and Dallas, and San

Antonio, and Atlanta. I don't know if they'll come back in two weeks or two years but they will be back, even those who are very angry right now, they'll come back because the way we feel about one another is just not the way people feel about each other out there in the rest of America. Maybe they'll make a little money for the first time, out there in America, but then they'll come back and use it to make things better here.

It's not blowing smoke when I tell you that we love each other that way. That's an actual fact of life in New Orleans. Everybody feels like they know you, like they are related, and, as a matter of fact, half of us at least are related in one way or another, through one family or another. We're a small city in a small state and everyone here is either kissin' kin or wants to be, like those of us who weren't born here but came long ago and couldn't bear to leave.

We don't always get along perfectly—sometimes we get off track and it takes a monumental event like Katrina to put everything back in perspective—but we truly care for one another just the same, and that, I think, is the secret of our charm, the thing that attracts others to us, that keeps our visitors coming back to New Orleans, this love of one another that we exude in the simplest ways. They are fascinated by it and want some of it.

We let people, our people and our guests, be themselves in New Orleans.

It's a *come as you are* kind of town, come as you really are or really want to be.

It doesn't matter where you live or who you are married to as long as one of you can cook, *come as you are.*

We adore our food, God, do we love our food. Everybody knows that, I am not telling you anything you don't already know. Ask me what my favorite dish is and I'll tell you flat out, "Anything cooked in New Orleans," as long as it doesn't have coconut in it. I am allergic to coconut, otherwise I would be eating those delicious coconut pralines, too.

We do know how to cook food, too. We have a law down here, you know. And that law is that if you can't cook, you have to leave . . . or at least marry someone who can cook. If you can't cook, you have to leave and take all of those prissy Teflon-lined pots and pans with you. They are of no use to *us,* you can believe me when I tell you *that.* We not only love to eat and to cook what we eat, we love to talk about what we are going to cook and what we are going to eat. Before we finish what we're eating, we're already talking about the next meal we're going to have together. Everybody cooks the same thing but everyone has a different recipe for making the same thing, so we never get tired of cooking it or eating it or just talking about it. I can hear those intense conversations now: "I love these red beans, how did you make them, I just love your red beans! Now, let me tell you how I make mine. Well, of course, you make a roux . . ."

And the beat goes on. Our music is always with us in our talk, in the way we walk—watch New Orleanians walking down the street, they're looser, sexier in their movements, because of the beat in their heads, the beat they acknowledge without even thinking about it, just moving with it. Our music is in the way we shake hands, and in the way we make a joyful noise to the Lord, and in the way we hug each other, the way we smile at one another, as if there is a sweet secret world and we each have a copy of the key that opens the door and lets us into that world. Music is our key to the good life.

The thing that makes music in New Orleans so special is that nobody anywhere else can play music like New Orleanians play it. It doesn't matter whether it's jazz, or blues, or rhythm and blues, or bluegrass—yes, even that, we even have really great bluegrass in New Orleans—or zydeco or that special thing we call the New Orleans Sound, which is part jazz, part boogie-woogie, part reggae, part salsa, and a whole lot of other stuff stirred in for good measure by the great masters such as Professor Longhair, Allen Toussaint, and my father, Charles Neville, and my uncles Aaron and Art and Cyril, and Ellis Marsalis, who taught so many of our young artists how to get it right.

All music is good, but when we play it, it's right. Like funk, for instance, we invented that, the Meters got it right from the very first note, and rap, New Orleans kids started that as childhood sidewalk games, played to while away the time, getting ready for their turn on top.

It doesn't matter whether we are shedding in our garages or sequined and tuxedoed up in Carnegie Hall, we can play it all—look at Wynton, burning up the classical scene.

Musicians and bands all over the world try to impersonate, I say impersonate, New Orleans musicians. I have heard them try, and some of them are real good, but they can't quite pull it off. New Orleans musicians, though, they can sit in and fit in no matter what the setting is, anywhere in the world.

I remember James Booker playing the music for the old silent films that they used to show at the Toulouse Theatre in the French Quarter when Russell Rocke had it, back when Russell and Vernel Bagneris were putting together *One Mo' Time*, that great musical about black vaudeville, back then. There was just this one man, playing one piano but, oh, my God in Heaven, the range of emotions he could inspire. When there was a train showing on the screen, he could make you feel that choo-choo tearing down the track, clickety-clack. When there was water on the screen, his music made you feel it sloshing all over you. He was like an entire orchestra all by himself.

New Orleans is, indeed, blessed when it comes to music.

It's got to be more than just the water we drink, the cayenne pepper we put all over everything we eat. We have so much more musical talent than any other place in the country or in the world, for that matter, and it just keeps coming, so it's got to be a gift. There's no other explanation.

God took his boots off to rest here because he liked the looks and the feel of this special place he had created, and then he saw the faith of the people and the love they had for each other. He wanted to hear music while he was resting in this special place, and, when he felt the faith of the people and the love they had for each other, he gave us the gift of music, and we have it in our souls for eternity.

and Lovers . . .

A Leafy Angel

To the Columns Hotel

Quietly at the corner table
where the dry fountain
drowns in unswept leaves
under its disconsolate angel,
the slim boy in the shadow
of the blooming *jeune fille*
has opened *Postmodern Art,*
a book. Twixt happiness
and unhappiness
the only break we get
she thinks is sleep.
Certain mental interiors
exist only in French
is what he thinks.
Stranger still she is chief thespian
in a play
taking place presently in her mind
where she does bad things
in order to build capital
for masturbation
with a visiting European

on whose shoulders
run little trains
powered by oblivion.
At the streetcar stop
an old woman in mourning black
watches her younger self run
alongside a mostly naked runner
following the streetcar line
to a perfect body.
They are Jasmine and Sweet Olive,
they have just met
in 1924 in The City
That Lives for Its Belles,
a bar.
Stranger, sit quietly here
this evening
at the Columns Hotel
on the terrace at dusk
where light goes out with flair
on froufrou and history.
Outside the body, happily,
begins the lie.

—ANDREI CODRESCU

This Isn't the Last Dance

RICK BRAGG

It has always had my heart in a box.

In the clip-joint souvenir shops in the gaudiest blocks of the Quarter, with canned Cajun music drilling rock-concert-loud into my ears, I could never resist opening the toy wooden coffins to see what was inside. I knew it would be just a cut-rate voodoo doll—a wad of rags, cheap plastic beads, and blind, button eyes. But every time, it made me smile. What a place, what a city, that can make you laugh at coffins and believe in magic—all the way to the cash register.

What a place, where old women sit beside you on outbound planes complaining about their diabetes while eating caramel-covered popcorn a fistful at a time. "It's hard, so hard, sweet baby," they will say of their disease, then go home and slick an iron skillet with bacon grease, because what good is there in a life without hot corn bread?

What a place, where in the poorest cemeteries the poorest men and women build tinfoil monuments to lost children in a potter's field, while just a few blocks over, the better-off lay out oyster po'boys and cold root beer and dine in the shade of the family crypt, doing lunch with their ancestors and the cement angels in cities of the dead.

What a place, so at ease here at the elbow of death, where I once marched and was almost compelled to dance in a jazz funeral for a street-corner conjurer named Chicken Man, who was carried to his resting place by a hot-stepping brass band and a procession of mourners who drank longneck beers and laughed out loud as his hearse rolled past doorways filled with men and women who clapped in time.

Now, for those of us who borrowed that spirit and used that love and then moved away, these past few awful days have seemed like a hospital death watch—and, in fact, for so many people it has been. And we stare deep into the television screen, at the water that had always seemed like just one more witch, one more story to scare ourselves into a warmer, deeper sleep, and we wonder if there is just too much water and too much death this time.

Ever since I was barely in my twenties, I have loved New Orleans the way some men love women, if that means unreasonably. I fell in love with the city and a Louisiana State University sophomore on the same night, eating shrimp cooked seven ways in the Quarter, riding the ferry across the black, black river where fireworks burned the air at Algiers Point. I drank so much rum I could sleep standing up against a wall. The sophomore left me, smiling, but the city never did.

There is no way to explain to someone who has never lived here why every day seemed like parole. Every time I would swing my legs from under the quilt and ease my toes onto the pine floors of my shotgun double, I would think, I am getting away with something here.

How long now before the streetcar rattles down St. Charles Avenue and beads swing into the two-hundred-year-old trees? How long before Dunbar's puts the chicken and stewed cabbage on the stove, or the overworked ladies at Domilisie's dress a po'boy on Annunciation Street, or the midday drinkers find their way back to Frankie and Johnny's on Arabella Street? Does my old house still stand on Joseph? It was high, high ground, on the lip of the bowl, and you could hit the Mississippi River with a silver dollar if you threw it twice.

I cannot stand the idea that it is broken, unfixable. I look at the men using axes to hack their way into hundred-year-old houses to save people trapped there by the suffocating water. I know there is life and death to be fought out for a long, long time. But I can't help but wonder what will come, later.

My wife, as wives do, voiced what most of us are afraid to say.

"I'm glad you took me there," she said. "Before."

We went there on our honeymoon.

Just a few weeks ago, I spent a week there, walking along Magazine, walking the Quarter, not minding the heat because that is what the devil sends, heat and water, to make you appreciate the smell of crushed cherries and whiskey on the balcony at the Columns Hotel, to make you savor the barbecued shrimp, to make you hear, really hear, the sound of a twelve-year-old boy blowing his heart out into a battered trumpet by a ragged cardboard box full of pocket change.

How long before that city reforms? Some people say it never will.

But I have seen these people dance, laughing, to the edge of a grave.

I believe that, now, they will dance back from it.

Cabaret Stories

Elizabeth Dewberry

I'm walking down Bourbon Street with a woman who dances at Rick's Cabaret. She's got big brown hair, big brown eyes. She's pretty, but in an ordinary sort of way. She's wearing a simple floral-print dress. She's not turning heads.

I want to understand why men go to these clubs, why women work at them. It's for a novel I'm trying to write.

"It's not about sex," she says. "If you think it's about sex, it'll mess with your head and you won't last two weeks. There's a high turnover. You have to remember that it's about fantasy. It's desire. People can live without sex, but you can't live without fantasy."

It's nighttime, but Bourbon Street is bright as neon. She usually works during the day, she tells me, when it's more laid back. "The later it is at night, the younger and drunker and cheaper the crowd is. They don't get it. They just want beer and tits. But during the day, it's men who want to see a pretty girl and talk to her. And you don't even have to be that pretty. Some days I look at myself and I think I can't do this, I'm too fat, my hair is too frizzy, whatever. But they don't really care. For a guy who walks into the club, it's about being in a place where any girl he sees wants to talk to him, wants to know his name. It's more important to make eye contact than to be beautiful. You've got to make that kind of connection. You can make a good living, but you've got to know you're not going to do this until you die. There's a girl who's been dancing for twenty years. She's raised two kids, bought a house in Metairie. But I don't want to do it much longer."

"What do you want to do?"

"I'm writing a book. I've already got an ISBN number."

We pass a street musician, a tenor saxophonist shaping sounds like wishes.

I don't tell her she doesn't need an ISBN for an unwritten book. She's not asking my advice.

"I've got so many stories," she says. "That's another reason they go there. They want to tell somebody their story."

The next afternoon, I go to Rick's. When she sees me, she rushes over to me and unfolds a photocopied piece of paper—a copy of her application for her ISBN.

"I'm going to do it," she says. "I'm not going to be here when I'm forty-five."

The DJ calls her name—it's time for her set—and she's still holding the paper. She folds it up like a dollar bill and tucks it into her garter as she walks up the stairs onto the stage.

Ella Fitzgerald is singing "Isn't It Romantic?"

Some people don't get New Orleans. They think Mardi Gras, for example, is all about breasts and beer. But New Orleans is about fantasy. It's about desire and awareness of mortality. It's a collection of stories, most of which will never be written.

It's Magic

PAUL PRUDHOMME

We talk a lot about magic at K-Paul because we believe in it, especially that old magic that we love so well, the soul of the people.

New Orleans is a great city because it nurtures that indefinable essence which drives us to identify ourselves, to delve deep into our souls and discover that thing in life which puts us on an emotional roll. And that emotional roll in turn is the magic which drives us to be ourselves.

We used to have a young guy working for us. He was a good employee and he worked for us a long time, until he had a problem and he couldn't be on his feet anymore. With us, he was easygoing, dependable, hardworking, the perfect employee, really, but he was quiet, didn't have a lot to say at all, was very retiring. I had the shock of my life the first time I saw him playing the saxophone. I literally did a double take because he was letting it all hang out, letting loose, going wild, playing fantastic music. And he was looking up like he was looking to heaven and he was smiling. He was doing what made him come alive, he was on a soul roll to beat the band.

New Orleanians get emotionally high on whatever

we love doing, whether it's cooking or going out to eat at a restaurant, playing music or listening to it, cheering for a football team (that can't seem to win for losing), scrambling around on our knees in the streets like maniacs for a handful of cheap plastic Mardi Gras beads, yelling, "Throw me somethin', mistuh!"

I found out a few years ago when I was a member of the faculty for the Faulkner Society's festival that William Faulkner didn't know he wanted to be a novelist when he came to New Orleans in the '20s. He thought he was a poet when he got to town but deep down he knew there was something else he wanted to do, to be. When he got in with the literary and social crowd here, people gave him the little nudges, the little gentle touches he needed, and the first thing you knew he was writing a novel. And you know what? I bet he smiled some after he figured out what it was that he just simply had to do to get his emotional high. He sure wrote a lot of books after that anyway. New Orleans is like that.

It nudges you to be what you need to be.

I'm a good example.

I was born near Opelousas, Louisiana. I had twelve brothers and sisters. And we didn't have a lot of money but Mamma and Daddy had figured out ways for us to be happy anyhow. My mamma was a born cook and she liked having me mess around in the kitchen, so I got a feel for handling food and pots and pans when I was very young. I had a restaurant there when I was seventeen. Got the jukebox company to put me in business and put their jukebox in the place. I got married at the same time. Nine months later I didn't have a wife—it was too much for her—and I didn't have a restaurant either. . . . I didn't know what I was doing really.

After that, I decided to try my luck in Colorado and worked in Vail when it was practically nonexistent. I had a few restaurants out there. Some of them failed. Two of them made a profit. But I was just cooking. It was just a job cooking the kind of food other people wanted me to cook. I had not yet been inspired to take control of the food, do my own thing.

Then I came to New Orleans.

The best thing I ever did was move to New Orleans. I had some false starts here, too, like the cooking school I started with my friend Terry Flettrich, which was kind of an inside joke with New Orleanians who knew that Terry never professed to be a cook. She was great on TV, though. That was the thing that made *her* heartstrings go *zing, zing, zing!*

I began to hit my stride during the five years I was with Ella Brennan at Commander's Palace. She taught me a lot, not just about cooking, but about running a restaurant and, especially, taking care of the front of the house, getting the people in and making them happy while they were there, so they would want to come back, of course.

After five years, I knew I had to be my own man to do exactly what I wanted to do. So I gave notice that I would be leaving to start my own place. I was married again by then and my wife, K, opened the place for us first for breakfast, then lunch. K was the "K" in K-Paul. During the time I was working out my notice, we discovered that without dinner we would not be able to make the restaurant work financially, and of course that's what I wanted to do. So we made our plans for a restaurant built on the concept of the kind of cooking I loved, down-and-dirty mamma cooking.

It's what people were longing for. Comfort food that tasted like Mom made it.

It's what I was longing to do, give them Mom's good food.

And, once I got it going, that emotional high going, it has never left me.

New Orleans did that for me, and I get a charge out of giving back by making people smile when they taste my food.

I am continually recharging, of course.

To date, I have been to thirty-five cooking schools around the world, and I get a huge emotional charge out of watching these chefs work with ingredients I have never used. Each time I go to a new school I pick up an idea for the reinvention of some of my standby dishes.

For instance, when I went to a Chinese cooking school I got a taste for ginger and sesame. I put a touch of ginger and sesame in certain dishes and these recipes got a new lease on life too!

People responded to the K-Paul's concept of food with enthusiasm at first, I believe, because down-home, down-and-dirty mamma's food in a fine-dining neighborhood such as the French Quarter was a novelty. They have remained loyal, however, because the dishes we serve are made with only the best and the freshest ingredients. *Debris* in the past was made with the shredded ends of roast beef, placed on a po'boy French loaf and covered with gravy. There was nothing wrong with the original dish, of course. We just raised the bar, however, by always making it with the best filet mignon. My cost for enough meat for a plate of *debris* is $3.50 per serving, *my* cost. I don't care, I will keep serving it even if I don't make any money on it because it is good and people love it.

Everything has to be fresh. *Only* fresh. We don't even have a freezer at the restaurant. The only freezer we have in our business is over at Magic Seasoning Blends, because some of our customers prefer to have their smoked meats (andouille and tasso) frozen before they are shipped. Tasso is cured meat, of course, and does not have to be frozen. But those crazy people out there in the rest of the country don't think it's fresh unless they get it frozen!

Sometimes I suspect that some of my staff have hidden freezers underground and are storing food there so we can cut costs and make more money. They assure me I am wrong, and certainly I have not been able to find one . . . yet. But if you see me digging up the sidewalk in front of K-Paul or ripping up one of the floors inside, you'll know I'm looking for a freezer. And you can rest assured that when I find it, I'm going to throw it out.

People enjoy our food not only because it is fresh, of course.

New Orleanians and their guests expect nothing short of magic, and that's what we give them when we put a dish in front of them prepared with the magic of patient cooking and the emotional charge of individuals who have identified what it is that they need to do to make them happy.

What It Means to
Miss New Orleans

Mark Childress

September 1, 2005.

ALL week we've been watching the immersion of a great old city. We imagine another city, less peculiar, will arise in its place. But I have this feeling it will never be quite the same nontoxic gumbo again.

For outsiders New Orleans was a place to party and eat food that is way too rich.

For the folks who live there it's more complicated—it's home.

Eighty-five percent of them were born there, and they're not going anywhere permanently, so forget this idea that they're going to move the city somewhere else. It's not going to happen. New Orleans is the opposite of America, and we must hold on to places that are the opposite of us. New Orleans is not fast or energetic or efficient, not a go-get-'em, Calvinist, well-ordered city. It's slow, lazy, sleepy, sweaty, hot, wet, lazy, and exotic.

I had a house there, up until three weeks ago, when I sold it. My friends say I'm lucky. I don't feel lucky.

Here are twenty-two reasons America needs New Orleans, the national capital of eccentricity:

1. The turtle soup at Galatoire's is presented in a white porcelain tureen, then ladled into your bowl by a waiter who reveals with a wicked smile that the turtle's name was Fred.

2. The hats in Fleur de Paris, a shop on Royal Street, are perfectly frivolous and ridiculous, beautiful visions of silk and lace.

3. Nowhere else in the country do so many Roman Catholic churches coexist peacefully with so many voodoo shops.

4. If you are a grown man, this is the only place in America where you can step off an airplane and be guaranteed that within thirty minutes a respectable woman unknown to you will call you "baby," as in "How you doin', baby!" If you are a grown woman, you will be called "darlin' " whether you are the least bit darlin' or not.

5. The beads of sweat on the unlined face of the conductor on the St. Charles streetcar.

6. Mardi Gras beads, but only the ones you catch, thrown by an actual masker on a float. The ones that hit the ground don't count unless they bounced off your hand or arm first.

7. The Lucky Dog is a venerated local frankfurter that has come a long way, culinarily speaking, from the days when Ignatius J. Reilly peddled them to tourists

in *A Confederacy of Dunces*. Now they are really good, especially if it is 4 a.m. and you are hungry.

8. I once met Thelma Toole, mother of John Kennedy Toole, author of *A Confederacy of Dunces*, who asked if I would buy her a "very expensive meal at the finest restaurant." This lady rolled her Rs like an 1860s stage actress to indicate her intellectual superiority to the rest of us. I took her to the restaurant of her choice, and by evening's end she had all the waiters gathered at our table, spellbound by stories of Kenny. "My son was a genius with a large and oddly shaped head," she boomed. Imagine what other great books Kenny might have written, she said, had he not killed himself in a car on that beach in Biloxi.

9. Every Twelfth Night, Henri Schindler, a local historian and Mardi Gras curator, holds a magnificent masked ball on the second floor of the Napoleon House, at the corner of Chartres and St. Louis Streets. White curtains blow in and out of the large empty rooms as masked figures glide past on a cushion of mystery.

10. Locals go to the Maple Leaf and Tipitina's to hear music. Also to Frenchmen Street, a cluster of ten or twelve small bars and clubs featuring, on any given night, ten or twelve kinds of music, about eight of which will be funky. (The other four will be too loud.) Usually at the better places there's a Neville involved, or a Marsalis.

11. My friend Martha Ann Samuels, a real estate agent,

revealed to me the actual location of Stanley and Blanche's house on Elysian Fields Avenue, a secret she learned from Tennessee Williams himself. (I'm not telling.)

12. Oyster loaf at Casamento's on Magazine Street. The crunchy local French bread showers crumbs on your hands. Each bite contains bread, mayo, and the delectable local bivalve, breaded and brilliantly fried. Casamento's closes down for the summer because oysters are better other times of the year.

13. At Jazz Fest, citizens happily stand in long lines in the blazing sun for a chance to eat crawfish bread, white boudin sausage, and alligator gumbo to the thump of Rockin' Dopsy from the Congo Square stage. (Could someone please put the Jazz Fest committee in charge of the Superdome?)

14. You can stand at the foot of Ursulines Avenue and watch a huge oceangoing ship slide by above the level of your head.

15. Along the promenade where the river passes Jackson Square, tourists still fall for one of the oldest New Orleans scams. A friendly fellow proposes that for a dollar he can tell you where you got them shoes. When you accept the bet, he says, "You got them shoes on your feet!" He keeps the dollar.

16. It has the only airport named for a jazz trumpeter, the indelible Louis Armstrong.

17. In the Confederate Museum near Lee Circle is a crown of thorns said to have been woven by Pope

Pius IX himself and sent as a gift to Jefferson Davis while he was imprisoned shortly after the Civil War. For me this artifact represents the height of Southern absurdity, and must be preserved for those future generations who will not believe it.

18. Every Thursday night at Donna's on Rampart Street, Tom McDermott plays the fastest, wildest ragtime, Brazilian, and stride piano you've ever heard. It's scary how fast his fingers move when he gets going. His feet come up off the floor.

19. Rich people live on the high ground. Poorer people live on the low ground. Recently some of the rich folks' houses got wet too.

20. Piety Street is one block over from Desire. Not a long walk at all.

21. On a foggy night the moon grows fat and full, and hangs in the sky above the big old river. It pours light on the water and makes a magical brown glitter that doesn't exist anywhere else. The water is the reason the city is there. The full moon pulls the tides into Lake Pontchartrain.

22. The city's sanitation department is considered among the finest in the nation. Its work during Mardi Gras is legendary. Can we please get this water out of here so they can get to work on this mess? The sooner the better.

The Second Stage of Passion

JULIA REED

To fly into New Orleans is to realize how utterly different—how strange—the place really is. When I was a kid in the Mississippi Delta, we always made the five-hour trek south by car, a fairly smooth transition, aided tremendously by a leisurely catfish lunch in Manchac, a tiny fishing village in the swamp below one of the two endless causeways that finally eased us into town. But on a plane there is no such transition. The chilly compartmentalized air is replaced by suffocating blasts of humidity that hit you as soon as you step onto the jetway, and the light is suddenly yellow and murky. It's discombobulating, like when you land in the Caribbean with too many winter clothes on and a watch set to the wrong hour, except that it's far, far more surreal. Upon my own first arrival, I was met by dozens of crawfish skittering along the hallways mostly unnoticed, and for a few long minutes I didn't realize that there was an explanation, that they were escapees from a tourist take-home box.

"It's the juxtapositions that get you," wrote Willie Morris about the South, and nowhere is that more true than in New Orleans. Think "jazz funeral" or "drive-through daiquiri shops." One of my first apartments was behind a cathedral school and in between two of the city's biggest gay bars, so that I was awakened by an off-key nun singing "My Country, 'Tis of Thee" every morning, and lulled—sort of—to sleep at night by the bass beat of "I Will Survive." When Tammy Wynette died, the bars played dueling versions of "Stand by Your Man" for a week. The Whitney Bank is still so old-fashioned its overdrawn notices have the feel of apologetic notes, but I have yet to stand in line at its French Quarter branch with fewer than two transvestites, and once I was transfixed by the famous behind of legendary Bourbon Street entertainer Chris Owens. It was directly in front of me and apparently had been lifted so many times that it rested in a spot very close to the small of her back.

Walker Percy wrote fondly of his briefly adopted city's "strange sightings" (afraid of becoming a slightly precious Quarter "patio dweller," he fled after a year or so, across Lake Pontchartrain to the relative normalcy of Covington, but he set two of his novels, *The Moviegoer* and *Love in the Ruins,* in New Orleans). "There it is," he wrote, "a proper enough American city and yet the tourist is apt to see more nuns and naked women than he ever saw before." I saw a naked man once on the corner of my block on Bourbon Street at five-thirty in the afternoon. He was drunk, trying rather pathetically to taunt—or maybe to interest—the patrons on the balcony at Lafitte's-in-Exile, but they turned out to be more interested in each other, and on the street not a single car slowed down to look.

You see enough of this stuff and before long, it's everywhere else that seems weird—or at least a lot more puritanical. When I was still dividing my time between New Orleans and Manhattan, I had put off buying the wine for a close friend's important birthday dinner before remembering, too late, that I couldn't buy it on Sunday. I'd been in New Orleans almost ten years by then and this was anathema to me. It is possible, at every hour of every day, to find alcohol—in one of the 1,500-plus licensed barrooms, in grocery stores and drugstores, at the aforementioned drive-throughs, and at stands set up on the sidewalk, since not only is it possible to drink and drive, it is also possible to drink and walk, in public.

It must be said that drinking is certainly a big help when it comes to softening some of the city's more startling juxtapositions, but there are plenty of other factors that lull you into an easy acceptance of almost everything. There is the heat, of course, and the fact that we have no seasons to speak of—even in the "winter" the vegetation stays lush and tropical so that it is often hard to keep track of time. Lunches morph into dinners, no one is ever in a hurry. Tennessee Williams wrote of the frequent rainy afternoons in which "an hour isn't just an hour but a piece of eternity dropped into your hands."

As usual Williams got it right—I think it's the peculiar quality time takes on in New Orleans that accounts above all for its reputation as one of the most romantic cities in the world. It's not the jasmine or the river or even the architecture, but the fact that being here almost always feels like being in what Robert Penn Warren identified (in *A Place to Come To*) as the second stage of a love affair—the best one, the one in which the world falls away and time stands still or ceases to move laterally, and more than anything else there is enormous contempt for the rest of the world.

No wonder Williams called the city where he lost his virginity his "spiritual home."

The hardest I've ever fallen was not long after my first surreal landing, and later it was hard to tell if I'd fallen for the man or the city, or the man because of the city. The greatest love song inspired by New Orleans is, after all, not about longing for a particular lover, but for New Orleans itself. Most of us do "know what it means to miss New Orleans," and it can be hard to endure. To leave is an escape back into real time, into an orderly landscape where the sightings are mundane rather than strange, where naked people cause a fuss, and rain is an irritating reason to reach for an umbrella. And no one who has ever experienced Penn Warren's second stage of passion has ever wanted to leave for that.

Carlotta's Vases

PATRICK DUNNE

How does this city take hold of your soul? Through a song or carnival parade or stolen kisses against the cool iron fence behind the cathedral with scent of sweet olive swirling around you. All these things would eventually have their clenching effect on me but first it was a pair of vases in my grandmother's South Texas house. Whipped into a Bernhardt moment by an appreciative audience, she would lead the captive, preferably a cub Irish priest just out, on a little tour of her rooms. The narrative, part family tree, part local history, was liberally sauced with humor and unself-conscious whimsy. I knew the script well but still found the climax thrilling. That came when she would gesture gracefully toward a pair of monumental vases with gilt and Pepto-Bismol pink decoration, draw in a breath, and with infinite melancholy pronounce that these were from NEW OR-LEANS and once belonged to dear tragic mad Empress Carlotta.

The effect of madness, tragedy, empresses, and New Orleans was so fabulously electric it always left me light-headed. I was determined one day to explore the same streets on which tattered royal mourning skirts were trailed. Sometime later this impulse was incongruously wedded to early Elvis Presley and the hot images of *King Creole*. I knew by heart the words to "Trouble" but it was the dawn street scenes of vendors chanting "crawfish!" that stole my heart. In the end Life does imitate Art. My first apartment was as much as possible like the film set. It had high rooms with a balcony hanging over Royal Street, where at any time of day or night one might spy tragic queens dragging their finery along the banquette, a local word for sidewalks. And if crawfish and callas were no longer being sold from carts in early morning, café au lait still steamed on cracked marble tables at the end of the French Market. Burgundy Street still had households of Creole courtesans of color, whose families went back to before the Civil War. And it was not so rare to find sidewalks or stoops "Xed" in terra-cotta chalk made of chipped-off brick from Marie Laveau's tomb. Laveau, a nineteenth-century hairdresser, was revered as Voodoo's highest priestess. The Xes were feared or sought, and meant lovers would suffer or succumb or neighbors fall deathly ill. I quickly learned to step high over these markings lest the dust stick to my shoe or soul.

New Orleans then and now is spotted with corner stores that have a specialty and a special character at the counter. How many lessons waited there for neophytes. One block over Old Man Brocato confected his Italian ices. Only when the berries lay perfect in the market or the melons were divinely fragrant would he consent to make and sell his wares, and then only if you had some charm or knew a cousin in his vast family. This meant the ices were always in short supply, and one lived steeled against the real possibility of disappointment. "The strawberries ain't fresh, so we got no ice!" Impossible! The French Market had been a virtual blush from Ponchatoula strawberries just that morning. Finally I realized much depended on his mood, which could be dark if some under-forty damsel had spurned his three-tooth smile the day before. It was the time when, mouth watering for the cinnamon-and-chocolate-chip cookies he made on Thursdays, I was met with "No cookies today, the chocolata chips no fresh." One of the great lessons New Orleans teaches is resignation in the face of frustrated appetite. It's easy here, because so many senses are teased and so many desires come true each day.

People in hot climates seem to need spicy food and many festivals. Who knows why—it's something New Orleans never questions. There's a huge secret here. We only survive because at least there is a little Lent, otherwise we'd simply wear ourselves out. But even the church can't really give in to forty whole days of abstinence. High in the season of penitence we break in mid-March to parade and sing and dance in the street and kiss pretty girls and boys on St. Patrick's and St. Joseph's Days.

The enervation here certainly must come from the intensity of light and colors. Partially it is Carnival's gold and purple that makes us unafraid of brilliant palettes and deeply scornful of safe cream and beige. It is also due to nature with its terrifying green of lush leaf growth sprawling across patios, reaching over walls and through gates, between the cracks in plaster and even carpeting the slate roof of the French Market in midsummer. It's a green that with little encouragement could swallow you up forever.

The exuberance of sun, the fierceness of sudden rainstorms even when one is sheltered under a deep balcony, the dangers posed by a sullen lake and unpredictable river all give our days and our relationships an ardor that is not found in many places. It is a city where there are enough stories to fill a thousand and one nights. If this is unable to keep the furies at bay, fury itself is turned into a song, a legend, or a spell.

Sometime after settling into my King Creole apartment I walked into the city's oldest antiques store. After the amiable chatter that is part of most New Orleans negotiations, I suggested that the vases my grandmother so treasured might have come from this place. "Oh!" the plump and highly amused dealer drawled. "Back then my grandfather sold a dozen pair of those every year." I went away sorry for all those who ended up with counterfeits, and very glad my grandmother had really managed to get hold of Carlotta's vases. Otherwise I might have never gotten here.

Portrait of the Artist

JULIE SMITH

Lee is the first to spot her. "You won't believe how beautiful this is," he says. "Come and look. My God, I wish I could paint."

The woman he sees is painting, but he doesn't mean he wishes he could paint like she can. He wants to paint *her*.

What he sees is the view from our window, which is on the third floor of an old building in the section of town called the Faubourg Marigny, or "the Faubourg" to the old-timers, though the rest of us call it the Marigny. We live in a loft reminiscent of a bowling alley, more New York than New Orleans except for the prevailing funk, which extends to the neighborhood as well.

The Marigny is just downriver from the French Quarter. If you cross Esplanade at Decatur to get to our block, you fetch up at a bar called Checkpoint Charlie, on the border of the two 'hoods. We live about fifty feet down Frenchmen Street.

Sharing our building are the Hookah Café, an Indian joint popular with the local hipsters, and Mona's, a Middle Eastern restaurant run by Palestinians. Within two blocks are two Thai restaurants, a sushi bar, a Mexican restaurant staffed by a German chef, an Italian place, and a soul food emporium. Only at the last will you find gumbo. We probably have the finest collection of ethnic restaurants in the city.

And we have clubs. There's Snug Harbor (where Ellis Marsalis and Charmaine Neville are regulars), the Spotted Cat (Washboard Chaz and the Jazz Vipers), d.b.a. (another hipster joint), the Blue Nile, and Café Brasil. Sprinkled in are a few neighborhood services— the gay bookstore our friend Otis runs, the Korean deli where Christy the cashier knows every regular by name and what he's going to order for lunch, Bicycle Michael's, and the tattoo place. Oh, and we have coffeehouses, my favorite being Café Rose Nicaud, run by neighborhood stalwarts Melba and Ken Ferdinand, who named it after one of our earliest entrepreneurs, a slave who peddled coffee at the French Market on her day off.

And that's still all in a two-block area. The residents live above the businesses, just like in Creole days. Stretching out, most of the neighborhood consists of single-family houses. People say the Marigny's "like the Quarter used to be" before the massive condoization, gentrification, and predominance of earsplitting late-night ghost tours. Elysian Fields, where Tennessee Williams housed the Kowalskis, runs right through it.

It's the kind of place where you can still afford to live if you're a waiter or a housecleaner or an artist, if you look hard for a good deal. What Lee sees from our window is something you might have seen fifty years ago, maybe even seventy.

It's an open window, the ten-foot kind you throw open from the floor and step through to get to the balcony. At the floor-to-ceiling window, opening onto the balcony, sits a woman at an easel, a young, dark-haired woman in a dress, cross-legged on the floor, so absorbed in her work she never seems to feel our eyes on her. The deep teal of the room behind her gives the scene the soft painterly quality that has so moved my husband. From time to time, she licks her brush, and sometimes she smokes.

We take to watching her at all hours of the night, just to see if she's still up, and because the scene is so breathtaking. Once, when we have guests, we turn out our lights so she won't catch us staring, and show her off. We're dying to see what she's painting, but we draw the line at binocs. We've already gotten too weird about this.

We just know we'd love her. She's so independent, so intrepid, such a serious artist.

One day I see her at the Frenchmen Deli and want to introduce myself, but I'm too embarrassed—maybe she'll think we're perverts or stalkers. Lee's bolder—when he runs into her, he tells her how beautiful she is when she paints, and, miraculously, she doesn't call 911. He asks her to come for a drink one day, but the hurricane comes before we can arrange it.

While we're in exile, we worry about her. Did she

try to ride it out? Did she get out safely? And one day she e-mails. Yes, she's safely out, but she's worried about us.

Next, we worry that she won't come back.

But then she e-mails again. She's dropped us a note from an Internet café, as if she doesn't have enough to do, with no power and no water, no open restaurants or markets. She *is* back, and we were right about the kind of person she is—she's sneaked in before the official okay.

The Street

Harry Shearer

When I think about New Orleans, the first things that come to mind are sounds: the music in the streets, the harmonious cacophony of the riverboat's just-out-of-tune calliope and the train's major-sixth whistle, a whistle that, at least as it goes by a mile away, sounds more hopeful than mournful. Then come the smells—the olfactory gumbo that greets me when I open my front door and relates what a quarter-million folks are cooking that day for lunch, mixed with the odor of old buildings taking their next gingerly step toward decay. But when that involuntary smile crosses my lips— the one that hits me so often at the recollection of New Orleans moments—it's more often than not associated with the little thoroughfare that my friend Kimball and I have taken to calling the Street.

Like so many of the streets in the city, especially in the French Quarter, the Street is a challenge to outsiders. Most of them—Burgundy, Conti, Chartres—pose their challenge in terms of pronunciation. If you weren't born there, you have no idea which names have been given absolutely whimsical local locutions, and which—and there are some—remain faithful to their antecedents.

But the Street challenges with its spelling: Its formal name is Frenchmen Street, and most folks assume they've seen a typo and pronounce it as if it refers to a singular Gallic male. But the name is officially, resolutely plural.

Frenchmen meanders across one end of the Faubourg Marigny, a largely gay neighborhood that's the next community downriver from the Quarter, a district that shares much of the Quarter's architectural character at (what used to be) a fraction of the price. As the centuries turned, Frenchmen began gathering a critical mass of little nightclubs—storefronts or double storefronts—until in the middle of the decade, Kimball and I could find each other strolling the Street most midnights, sampling the musical buffet, tipping each other off as to who was particularly good where.

What the Street has offered, in addition to quantity, is a grand stylistic variety: jazz, reggae, traditional jazz, Latino, Brazilian, modern rock—almost everything except the large-band funk that predominates at the bigger, better-known clubs and the old soul covers that are familiar primarily to denizens of that other street, the one with the less welcoming smells, the one called Bourbon. Some nights, I'd be one of three patrons at the bar while a local bluegrass band (yes, there is one) showed me just how many different kinds of music can be proud to call New Orleans home. Other nights, in the thick of Jazz Fest, I'd stand safely outside a club clotted with sweaty visitors dancing the night away to music that was born decades before they were. It's a New Orleans tradition to leave club doors open, so people in search of fresh air and room to move can still hear the music.

And Frenchmen draws resonance, like so many streets in New Orleans do, from memories of other great times in the place: the Krewe de Vieux parades that, two and a half weeks before Fat Tuesday, punctuate Carnival season with a nonmechanized cavalcade of floats, down Frenchmen and into the Quarter, emphasizing the raunchy and the savagely satirical; or nights like the one at Snug Harbor, the jazz club, when Johnny Adams, the Tan Canary in the final year of his life, sang with piano genius Henry Butler, sang with such fierce intensity that you knew it was a performance Adams intended you to remember for the rest of your life. It gets resonance, too, from the clear awareness, even before the recent events, that its life might be foreshortened: signs have sprouted in the middle of the Street announcing the construction of grand new condominiums, and every sentient patron of the clubs knows that means a day will come when people who paid too much for their condos will start complaining about "the noise."

For now, I look on the Web, and on the list of clubs that have survived the storm are most of the spots on the Street. It looks as if there will be more nights when, sated with the food and unwilling to call it a night, I'll wander the few blocks to Frenchmen and let the musical lottery decide what I win.

Taking Yansa to See Miss Marie

(with Apologies to the Shade of Jorge Amado)

JESSICA B. HARRIS

Now, I have many tales of the happenings in the magical city at the bend of the big muddy river, some culinary, some fanciful, all savory. My favorite among them is of the day that I took Yansa, the Yoruba *orixa*, or goddess, of the precincts of the cemeteries, commerce of the marketplace, and of whirlwinds and tempests (and, yes, hurricanes) to St. Louis Cemetery Number One to visit her sister in spirit Marie Laveau.

It happened on a day in June at the French Market, during the Tomato Festival, which celebrated the arrival of the succulent, weighty, ruby globes we call Creole tomatoes. The weekend had begun with a parade led by my friend Lou Costa in his tomato red tails and had continued with a one-day symposium extolling the virtues of the tomatoes in the foods of the Creole world (my reason for being there). It ended with cooks from various points on the Creole compass serving up favorites from their menus for crowds who strolled through the market and the shops. My Brazilian girlfriend Maria Elena, an initiated votary of Yansa Bale, the avatar of the *orixa* who owns the precincts of the cemetery, was in attendance serving the bean fritters known as *acaraje* that are one of her *orixa*'s ritual foods.

It was a Friday. On that day in Bahia, Brazil, a city that shares its love of magic and mystery with New Orleans, people who honor the ancient African spirits wear white in honor of Obatala, Lord of the White Cloth. Maria Elena, in her haste to pack for the unexpected trip, had forgotten this and found herself in the town with only multicolored vestments. Knowing her dilemma, I offered her my Bahian ritual clothing, a full white lace skirt that would have done Carmen Miranda proud topped with a blouse of intricate cutwork embroidery that would have made Ralph Lauren weep with delight. They were seriously impractical for cooking a dish that involves the staining red palm oil known as *dende,* but suitable for honoring the father of all *orixas.*

As I strolled by toward the end of her session, I was pleased to note nary an orange spot on my treasured clothing. She'd just finished up and was talking in sign language and broken English with one of the Haitian vendors who sold baskets at the market. As I approached, I could tell that they were talking about matters of the spirit and heard the Haitian woman ask Maria Elena what they would call her *orixa* in the *Vaudou* pantheon. With a twinkle that could have only been a glimmer of the trickster Ellegba, she opined that it might be Erzulie Dantor and began to hum a tune.

Spirit called spirit. Maria Elena's Yansa interrupted her business on the Bahian island of Itaparica, heeded the call of the *Vaudou* rhythms, and came dancing to our corner of the old French Market to mount her votary. Maria Elena had been eclipsed by the warrior spirit in the manner of Yoruba worship. I found myself face to face with the powerful *orixa*. I removed her shoes—I knew to do that much—and loosened her garments, still watching out for my drag. Yansa strutted proudly around a bit, savoring the feel of the market and clearly enjoying the river breezes of the late Louisiana afternoon. The Haitian lady and I were frantic, thinking of ways to make the imperious *orixa* return to her Bahian business, but she was clearly savoring her New Orleans sojourn. Finally, she agreed to leave if she could visit the cemetery.

Now, I knew of only one nearby cemetery in New Orleans, St. Louis Number One, where tourists and believers alike used to make their XXXs on the tomb of the Widow Paris, known to the world as Marie Laveau. With a quick explanatory word to a startled Lou, who blanched and warned of dire happenings at New Orleans cemeteries, and the help of Maria Elena's friends, who understood the matters of Bahia's capricious *orixas,* we were off.

I knew that rum wouldn't be a bad thing and a cigar might go well too, so we stopped at French Quarter Liquors, where I bought both. Then, I remembered, beans: the *orixa*'s favorite food . . . a second stop at a souvenir shop on Canal Street yielded a nine-bean soup mix that was too perfect to be an accident. (Nine is Yansa's ritual number and the mix included her totemic black-eyed peas!)

The sun was fading rapidly as we arrived only to discover that the gates had been closed and locked for the night. No matter. Yansa/Maria Elena's exit from the back of our tiny car had stopped the projects cold. Folk peered from their balconies and the group of B-boys lounging by their car turned their radio not only down, but *off!*

Slowly, with the deference due a powerful queen, I led Yansa to the gates of the cemetery and watched in amazement as in one graceful skyward leap and rustling unfurling of lace skirts, Yansa kept her promise and departed. My friend Maria Elena was back. She and I honored all the cardinal points of the cemetery with rum and smoke and small piles of beans, and returned to the car, which had been scrupulously guarded by all, who were full of questions. We answered a few and then returned to the market to assure Lou that we had accomplished our mission. As is usual with ritual possession, Maria Elena remembered nothing of her journey, but I have dined out on many an evening telling my story of how I took Bahia's Yansa to see New Orleans's fabulous Miss Marie.

When Worlds Collide

STEWART O'NAN

My New Orleans isn't real, not like my Pittsburgh. I was over thirty the first time I saw the city, from the roomy backseat of a limousine. I was drinking champagne with my wife after having won a prize for my first novel. In reality, at home, I was unemployed and writing in an unheated attic, so it was all a goofy dream. Buzzed, gliding by the giant silver spaceship of the Superdome, I felt lucky and glamorous, like Scott Fitzgerald at the beginning of his brief, dizzying affair with New York. That night I put on a tuxedo and bowed to Richard Ford so he could put a medal around my neck. After the reading and the reception, we partied deep into the morning, wandering back to our four-star hotel through the echoing, puddled streets of the French Quarter.

A day to remember, yet even as I enjoyed my good fortune, I understood it was a fantasy. I could take in the heat and stink of the streets but, like any tourist, I knew nothing of the actual city—the people who worked there and then went home to their families in literally hundreds of different neighborhoods and suburbs. And having grown up in Pittsburgh, I couldn't forget that for everyone out on the town that night, there were others working unfun, unglamorous jobs to make the party happen. Even half smashed, I knew that someone had to fix every drink, and wash every dish, and mop every floor, and take shit from a boss, and not for a lot of money.

That's a projection, partly due, I'm sure, to my own puritanical Pittsburgher guilt for not working while others are. I'm terrible at vacation, no matter where I go, and my own anxiety over how people get by goes against everything New Orleans—or any tourist town—stands for. In me, it's a knee-jerk response at first, replaced by a basic curiosity about how others live day-to-day. I want to follow the dishwasher home and see how he ends the night.

The tourist isn't here for that, but instead to forget real life and indulge himself or herself in whatever lavish pleasures the city offers, and New Orleans offers more than any city save perhaps Vegas. I'm not immune to those pleasures, not at all, which is why I'm happy to go back again and again, despite my anxieties.

I suppose I could move to New Orleans and learn the real city, but it would take years, and I still wouldn't feel it in my bones like a native. My New Orleans is made up of holidays and long weekends, meals eaten in restaurants and boozy late nights—sadly or not so sadly, depending on how deeply you want to look or feel. While the city and its people do their best to play host, I'll always be a tourist here, always trying to enjoy the fantasy while sneaking peeks behind the scenes.

Walking the Dog with Joe

Bret Lott

It's almost dinnertime, that event around which all other plans are built while in New Orleans. We have friends who say that they count their visits to the city not by how many days they will be here, but by how many meals they'll eat.

But no one will head out for dinner from Joe and Rosemary's house until Zuli has been walked, and so here are Joe and Zuli and I, heading out the heavy-paneled doors of the front hallway and onto slate-paved Pirate's Alley, just across it the beauty and mystery of the oak-shrouded garden behind St. Louis Cathedral.

Even before we've gotten fully into the alley, even before I've pulled the heavy door closed behind me, my wife, Melanie, and Rosemary staying inside to continue their talk of where we ought to eat *tomorrow* night—tonight, of course, has been decided long ago—people have stopped and looked at the dog, all of them smiling and cooing and reaching to touch. And Zuli has already swept the crowd, her eyes above them all, looking up the alley to where it lets into Jackson Square.

Zuli: Joe and Rosemary's standard poodle; a queen, regal in her silvery black fur cropped short save for the luxurious poof atop her head; the center, suddenly, of all the French Quarter.

Regal is the only word.

And it's this imperial bearing that guides us on the walk, a bearing to which people everywhere, *everywhere*, have no choice but to bow. First there are these tourists right here outside Joe and Rosemary's door, a half dozen sunburnt men and women wearing shorts and leather shoes, Mardi Gras beads stacked a dozen deep around their necks. They smile and talk of how beautiful this doggie here is, and how beautiful the French Quarter is, and how beautiful this alley is and this garden and this house we have just stepped out of, and now Zuli is off, and we are left to apologize to the tourists for Her Majesty's impatience.

Then we are at the corner café ten yards away, where a man in black leather and gray goatee and dark glasses, newspaper held out in front of him like a spy hiding from no one, lowers the paper, smiles over it and the empty coffee cup on the wrought-iron table in front of him, and says, "Hello, Zuli!" as though this might be his grandchild arriving right on time.

But Zuli moves on, moves on, and Joe waves a wave at the man, who only nods, lifts the paper to resume his incognito performance, and now we are even farther down the alley, about to step out into Jackson Square itself, and the hubbub that won't die down until sometime near dawn.

And now we are here, on the plaza in front of the cathedral in late-afternoon light, everything everywhere crystal clear and shadowed, all darkness and light, the sun already behind the cathedral and the Presbytere and the Cabildo. We head to the right and along the Pontalba, everywhere people continuing to pay obeisance to Zuli, strangers and friends alike: now the palm readers who are set up in their rickety chairs and even more rickety tables wave and say hello, smiling and smiling and smiling, and now street artists, their wares hung on the iron fence around the park, wave and say hello, and a busboy in a restaurant on the first floor of the Pontalba nods hello and calls out "Zuli!" and then the tourists at the table next to the one he buses call out, "Look at the poodle!" and smile and wave.

Joe and I try to talk books, to talk about writers, to talk about how the store is doing, how the journal is doing. We try to talk about all of this, but there is only one truth to our being out here on a beautiful late afternoon before heading out to dinner: we are walking Zuli, and I see like I do every time I ever walk the dog with Joe that Zuli is the star, and that Joe and I are merely her entourage.

It's like this the entire walk down the wide flagstone esplanade before the Pontalba, all the way to Decatur, where, as we cross with the light, people hang out of cabs and cars to look at her. Still she sweeps the crowds, her eyes above them all.

And still the late-afternoon sun behind the cathedral casts this all in shadow and light: the carriages lined up and waiting on Decatur, the ironwork on the balconies of the buildings, the palms and live oaks and magnolias in the park growing darker and sharper and cooler with that evening sun on its way down.

Then we are on the levee, before us the Mississippi itself, that fabled brown of it, the crescent of it sweeping away from us on either side, all of it in sunlight, the sun just above the buildings behind us for how high the levee is, and there seems something magical in this moment, in this most American of rivers at my feet, blazed in light about to disappear for the turn of the earth, and in the shadows that have already engulfed Jackson Square behind us, and in the history of this place, the tumult and triumph and pleasure and pain and music and literature and cuisine and culture, all of it, all of it on the face of a planet turning so fast that, while we stand there, shadows behind us are creeping up the levee, making ready to break out and onto that river, and to begin to swallow it all with the night fast upon us.

I am here in New Orleans, walking the dog with Joe.

"Look at the puppy!" someone says, and I turn to see Joe and Zuli already gone, headed to the left along the walkway atop the levee, another sunburnt tourist heaped with Mardi Gras beads bent to Her Royal Highness. Zuli merely sniffs at the tourist's hand as she saunters past, the world and all its considerations left in Zuli's wake.

Zuli, I see, in all her imperial bearing, all her presence and regal posture and beauty and carefree nobility, might as well be New Orleans herself.

And now I hurry to catch up.

Miracles of the Ordinary

Ron Shelton

It's an image from a couple years ago. Like the peasant Juan Diego who saw the Virgin of Guadalupe in Mexico or the woman who saw Jesus in a burrito in Texas, it's the image that matters. It's there and it's gone, and forever my miracle of the ordinary for New Orleans.

A Sunday morning at the corner of St. Philip and Bourbon, outside Lafitte's bar, amid the trash and piss of a Saturday night only now ending, I saw it. Why I was standing outside a bar I don't really like—they won't make Sazeracs "because it's a specialty drink," the barkeep snarls, "we don't like specialty drinks here"—is one of those questions that doesn't come up here. I have a home a block away, but that still doesn't explain why I would be there just standing, waiting for something.

And then it happened.

Walking south on Bourbon, toward me, were four large white men with neatly trimmed beards, talking intimately, finishing each other's sentences. Each was wearing a silver angel dress (calf high), each had a pair of silver angel wings that floated above his immense shoulders, and each had a silver halo bobbing above his head, held on by a concealed wire. A neat trick. And each wore silver heels of modest height that gave them enormous difficulty.

They were going to church, or something like church. The sun was out, their outfits were perfect and unwrinkled, their performance was perhaps moments away—and they were well-rehearsed and ready. They had the jitters of any performers about to go onstage. Who doesn't get butterflies? They were alive and they looked sharp and it was good.

And then, from my left heading east on St. Philip, four black girls, maybe ten years old, each in satin orange dresses made fresh for the occasion. Each with orange shoes, short heels, and four-inch-high bows of the same color in their hair. Singing, talking, working out harmonies from a long-practiced routine. Something about Jesus and the Cross and the blood shed for all of us. And the singing and the talk and the giggling all blurred together, going to church.

And the silver angels continued south and the little girls continued east and the girls passed right in front of the angels and disappeared toward the river and the angels continued past Laffite's and, then, were gone deep into Bourbon Street.

Neither group saw the other because there was nothing to see.

Two months after the deluge, I'm standing by Lafitte's. It's nine in the morning. The Quarter is empty, barely creeping back to life. There's still the debris of plastic cups and the smell of urine. The morning paper outlines yet again a flood-control plan of gates and higher levees and it's all old news and the authorities at every level seem frozen.

The church is closed, for now.

I want to order a Sazerac just to hear the barkeep snarl, but even Lafitte's isn't open. The oldest bar in the country, brought to its knees by someone named Katrina.

So I get in my car to drive to the east side. I want to see the worst of it up close. I have no idea what the city should do or the state or the feds or any damn body. The city should never have been here in the first place—it was the New World's first pork-barrel project, really, just a way for the explorer Bienville to finance his adventures by convincing Louis XIV that it was a great place for a military base to launch attacks on the Spanish Empire. It was a swamp and will always be a swamp.

It is one of the greatest things about the city—it shouldn't be here.

And every so often it burns to the ground or the river washes it away so it can find itself again in some way that can't be planned or mandated.

Or maybe it's over.

So, I drive out Esplanade toward the highway east and my eye catches something, peripheral, a blink, my heart seizes and I slam on the brakes. A boy runs across the street in front of my car, which stops inches from running him over. I'm trying to catch my breath. The boy doesn't stop running, hurrying with the urgency of a twelve-year-old.

The boy didn't know I almost hit him. He didn't hear the brakes. He saw nothing except where he was going. He was oblivious.

And he was carrying a trumpet.

Mr. Spaceman Arrives

ROBERT OLEN BUTLER

I move my hand and my spaceship descends, straight down, from twenty miles above Jackson Square in the French Quarter of New Orleans, Louisiana, to ten miles above to five to one and the ship is cloaked and invisible, and on the screen I see the crowd roiling in anticipation, for the millennium has only a little more than a minute left in it and I am coming, I am coming to you, planet Earth, you will soon understand, and I am half a mile above and a quarter mile and my hand now is poised to uncloak this craft and my body is roiling like the crowd, roiling with the heat of the stars that you creatures there below know only as tiny bits of ancient light, I fall to you, I fall and I move my hand now and I make the ship visible to everyone and beneath me is St. Louis Cathedral with three spires, the center one, the tallest, pointing straight up at this wondrous sight, this vessel from outer space. I place the craft on its automatic settings and quickly I glide to the center of the control room.

And I wait, stiffly, without "A Song in My Heart," and the light flares, fills my eyes, catches me tight, and I begin to sink down. I close my eyes and I try to "Whistle a Happy Tune," but my mouth is too rigid to pucker and I am free of the ship and I am in the night air and I open my eyes, there are corridors of light and blooms of fireworks and a steady roar of human voices beneath me and I look down and the high center spire is aimed right at me and I move my hand and adjust the beam and I slide out, and the square before the cathedral unfolds before me, teeming with life, and I am ready to see them, see all these faces turned up to me, to this extraordinary sight, a spaceman in a felt hat and gray suit with hot-sauce bottles floating on his tie coming down in a beam of light. I focus. I blink my big old spaceman eyes and I concentrate my superior vision and I am descending into a great sea of plumes and feathers and masks and I look harder as I descend and I am passing the highest tip of the spire and I descend toward an enormous pink rabbit—the Energizer battery bunny who "keeps going"—and a human Coke can, a face framed in the ring of the pull tab, and a woman warrior with plastic breastplates and brandishing an aluminum foil sword and a nearly naked King Neptune with trident and seashell jockstrap and a man shrouded in a great, full-body rubber sheath with French Tickler top and a gang of bikers in black leather but with great swaths of their jackets and pants missing, and I look more widely at the crowd and some faces are clearly focused on me, some hands point and wave, and I realize I am missing my opportunity, I am being the spectator not the show, and I wave in return and a trio of nuns, side by side, see me and they return my wave and then in unison they clap their hands against the center of their chests—it is the mea culpa, they feel they have sinned—and I am about to spread my hands before them, to offer them reassurance, but before I do, they all three open wide the fronts of their habits and expose their breasts—three pairs of pink, wondering eyes stare up at me—and the habits close and the nuns acknowledge the applause of those around them and they receive the kisses of the bikers and I am falling into confusion in this column of light and I scan the crowd, trying to understand, and suddenly I realize that I have won, at last, the attention of much of the crowd, I feel all eyes on me, and the nuns have taught me something—a precious lesson I should have learned already—I have dressed in my suit and shirt and tie, as if I were an Earthling myself—what a basic blunder I have made—and I rip off my hat and my tie, and my spaceman face, at least, is nakedly clear—I will not fail in what I must do—I heighten my voice to be heard far and wide and I do not plan what to say, I trust the words to come, and I begin, I am a friendly guy come from a distant planet. You are not alone. And though my voice is loud, the crowd is louder—they are not alone, they are one voice, uttering a sound like the sea, roaring in a storm—and I am descending further, getting closer and closer, but I sense the moment of all eyes being on me has passed, most of the eyes have remained where they were even as I have moved—in spite of my face being clearly visible now—

and I glance back and above me and it is the clock they were watching—and they still are—the new millennium is coming, only seconds away, and they are focused on this moment, on this moment in their senses, in the company of each other, and I look out at them and they are indeed a vast sea, they are moved by a great rising wave, all of them together, bunny and biker, Neptune and nun, Coke can and condom, they are one people, and I know why I have made my blunder, why I descended dressed as one of them, and I fall in my column of light past the great front doors of the cathedral and I know my own yearning clearly now, even as a man in ostrich feathers and a woman in combat fatigues press back against the crowd to make a place for me. And the crowd cries out, *Three, two, one!* And then there is a great roar and my eyes are full of tears and the wave lifts us all and I swim into the crowd hugging and being hugged, kissing and being kissed.

❈ ❈

I am. Still. I am more than ever. I sent the ship back to where it came from. I told my species to stay away for a century or two, at the very least. . . .

❈ ❈

I feel at home here. I work in Jackson Square. My colleagues are the fire-eaters and the jugglers and the painters and the fortune-tellers. I sit at a little table and my sign says *Talk with a Spaceman*. I do what I have always done. I listen to the voices of this planet, one at a time. I am a good listener. Some people think I really am a spaceman, an incarnate glimpse into the infinite and mysterious elaboration of the universe. Some people think I am just one of them in costume, an Earthbound creature caught in time and yearning his way along. Look around. Listen to each other. I am both, and so are you. So let's go around the corner, you and I, and get a flaming dessert together.

Lately I've been thinking there's a revelation to be had from a sweetly burning banana.

An Epilogue: Spice of Life

ROY BLOUNT, JR.

What holds multifarious old New Orleans together? I think it must be the seasoning. I had a New Orleans cabdriver once who said, "I don't like the food other places. It doesn't have seasoning."

Everything in New Orleans, not just the food, is highly seasoned. The air is full of smells and sounds and palpabilities deriving directly from the place and stretching way back into the place's history. Underfoot the streets feel deeply seasoned, and alongside the streets, the buildings look seasoned—they have been lived in, and they have been lived in with feeling.

People in New Orleans are seasoned, as in spicy and as in veteran. In New Orleans complete strangers will talk to you as if they know you, will call you Cher or Darlin' and let you in on what they're thinking, because they know who they are, from way back, and they assume you know who you are, and you both sure as hell know where you are, so why be standoffish? Partying breeds familiarity, and so does crisis.

Here is one dictionary definition of "season":

"To render competent through trial and experience."

And here are some words that *Roget's International Thesaurus* associates with "seasoning" and "seasoned":

Salty, racy, lively, savory, pungent, poignant, piquant, hot, tangy, lively, keen, gamy, brackish, pickled, marinated, sprinkling, taint, suggestion, dash, touch, smack, nip, relish, zest, vestige, mellowing, ripening, aging, experienced, inured, worldly-wise, modulated, habituation, adaptation, adjustment, familiarization, preservation, acclimation.

Not *weather-beaten.* That goes beyond seasoning. New Orleans has never been beaten by weather yet.

Contributors

Roy Blount, Jr., is the author of nineteen books, including *Robert E. Lee; Roy Blount's Book of Southern Humor; Feet on the Street: Rambles Around New Orleans; I Am the Cat, Don't Forget That;* and *If Only You Knew How Much I Smelled You* with photographer Valerie Shaff. Blount has had a long love affair with New Orleans, starting with a short stint as a reporter for *The Times-Picayune.*

Rick Bragg won the 1996 Pulitzer Prize in Feature Writing for his "elegantly written stories about contemporary America." Also a recipient of the Distinguished Writing Award of the American Society of Newspaper Editors, he was a reporter for *The New York Times* for many years. Additionally, he has written for *The Washington Post, Los Angeles Times, St. Petersburg Times,* and *The Birmingham News,* and magazines including *GQ.* Bragg is the author of *I Am a Soldier, Too; Somebody Told Me; Ava's Man;* and the bestseller *All Over but the Shoutin'.*

Ella Brennan, co-author with her brother Dickie Brennan of *The Commander's Palace New Orleans Cookbook,* has been called "the reigning Queen of New Orleans cuisine" by *People* and "the doyenne of New Orleans dining" by *Southern Living*. The acknowledged leader of café society in the Big Easy, she has won the Lifetime Achievement Award of the Southern Foodways Alliance, the Savoir Faire Award of the American Culinary Institute, the Lafcadio Hearn Award, and induction into the Culinary Institute's Hall of Honor. In 1966, under her leadership, Commander's was awarded the Lifetime Outstanding Restaurant Award from the James Beard Foundation and later the Lifetime Service Award. Her protégés include Paul Prudhomme, Emeril Lagasse, and, most recently, Jamie Shannon.

Poppy Z. Brite is a native New Orleanian and the author of numerous books, including *Lost Souls, Drawing Blood, Exquisite Corpse, Wormwood, Courtney Love: The Real Story, The Lazarus Heart, Are You Loathsome Tonight, Seed of Lost Souls, Plastic Jesus, Liquor, The Value of X, Prime,* and *The Devil You Know*. She lives with her husband, New Orleans chef Chris Debarr, in an old house in Uptown New Orleans.

Robert Olen Butler won the Pulitzer Prize for his collected stories, *A Good Scent from a Strange Mountain*. He is the author of *Had a Good Time: Stories from American Postcards, They Whisper, Tabloid Dreams,* and *Mr. Spaceman*. A recipient of the National Fiction Award, his stories have been included in four annual editions of *The Best Ameri-*

can Short Stories. Butler is the Francis Eppes Professor of English at the University of Florida in Tallahassee, where he lives with his wife, novelist and playwright Elizabeth Dewberry.

Leah Chase is proprietor of the renowned Dooky Chase Restaurant, a bastion of Creole cuisine and culture in New Orleans, founded in 1939 as a po'boy stand by her late husband, Edgar "Dooky" Chase II. Chase is the recipient of the Candace Award, the *Times-Picayune* Loving Cup Award, and the Lifetime Achievement Award of the Southern Foodways Alliance. Additionally, she has been inducted into the Lafcadio Hearn Hall of Honor and the Chef John Folse Culinary Institute.

Mark Childress is author of *Crazy in Alabama, A World Made of Fire, V for Victor, Tender, Gone for Good, One Mississippi,* and three books for children, *Henry Bobbity Is Missing, Joshua and Bigtooth,* and *Joshua and the Big Bad Blue Crabs.* Childress is a regular contributor to *The New York Times* and *Salon.* A native of Mississippi, Childress now lives in New Orleans.

Andrei Codrescu was born in Sibiu, Romania, emigrated to the United States in 1966, and became a U.S. citizen in 1981. He is the MacCurdy Distinguished Professor of English at Louisiana State University in Baton Rouge. He is the author of the novels *Wakefield, Casanova in Bohemia, Messiah, The Blood Countess,* and *The*

Repentance of Lorraine; the poetry collections *It Was Today, Alien Candor, Poezii Alese, Belligerence,* and *Comrade Past and Mister Present;* the memoirs and travelogues *An Involuntary Genius in America's Shoes (and What Happened Afterwards), Ay, Cuba! A Socio-Erotic Journey, Road Scholar: Coast to Coast Late in the Century,* and *Hole in the Flag: A Romanian Exile's Story of Return and Revolution;* and the essay collections *The Muse Is Always Half Dressed in New Orleans, Zombification: Essays from NPR,* and *A Craving for Swan.* He is the editor of *Exquisite Corpse,* an online literary journal. Codrescu divides his time between Baton Rouge and New Orleans.

Elizabeth Dewberry is the author of four novels, *His Lovely Wife, Sacrament of Lies, Break the Heart of Me,* and *Many Things Have Happened Since He Died,* and several plays, including *Flesh and Blood.* Her nonfiction has appeared in such places as *Southern Living, 21st,* and *The Cambridge Companion to Hemingway.* She lives outside Tallahassee, Florida, with her husband, Robert Olen Butler.

Patrick Dunne has lived in New Orleans for thirty-five years. The author of *The Epicurean Collector,* and senior editor-at-large for *House Beautiful,* he is the proprietor of Lucullus, an antiques store devoted to the arts of cooking and dining, favored by an international clientele of designers and collectors.

Randy Fertel, a native New Orleanian, teaches the Literature of Exile at the Graduate Faculty of the New School in New York City. Currently, he is finishing a family memoir, *The Gorilla Man and the Empress of Steak*. He is the head of the Fertel Foundation, which sponsors the Ron Ridenhour Awards for Courageous Truthtelling, and the Ruth Fertel Foundation, dedicated to education in New Orleans.

Patty Friedmann is a native and lifelong resident of New Orleans. She is the author of the novels *Secondhand Smoke, Odds, Eleanor Rushing,* and *Side Effects,* and of the memoir *Exact Image of Mother,* about growing up Jewish in New Orleans, and the humorous *Too Smart to Be Rich: A Satiric Look at Being a Yuffie.* Ms. Friedmann regularly writes for such publications as *Newsweek, Short Story,* and *Publishers Weekly.*

Roy F. Guste, Jr., is a native son of New Orleans whose forefathers arrived with Bienville, the French explorer who founded the city. Formerly fifth-generation proprietor of Antoine's Restaurant, founded by his great-great-grandfather Antoine Alciatore, Guste now devotes his time to writing and is the premier authority on Creole cuisine. The author of ten cookbooks, including *The Antoine's Cookbook, The 100 Greatest Dishes of Louisiana Cookery, The Restaurants of New Orleans, Gulf-Coast Fish, The Bean Book,* and *The Tomato Cookbook,* Guste's *The Secret Gardens of the Vieux Carré* and *The New Orleans Cookbook* are being reissued in 2006.

Jessica B. Harris, a native New Yorker and adopted New Orleanian who owns a home in the Bywater area of the Big Easy, is a culinary historian and the author of *The Welcome Table: African-American Heritage Cooking; Iron Pots and Wooden Spoons: Africa's Gifts to New World Cooking;* and, most recently, *Beyond Gumbo.* A regular contributor to *Food & Wine* and *The New Yorker,* she is the recipient of an appreciation award from Walt Disney World Epcot Center, the Heritage Award from the Black Culinarians, and the Food Hero award from *Eating Well* magazine. She is a professor at Queens College in New York City.

Walter Isaacson, a native New Orleanian, is the president and CEO of the Aspen Institute. He has been the chairman and CEO of CNN and the managing editor of *Time* magazine. Mr. Isaacson is the author of *Benjamin Franklin: An American Life* (2003) and of *Kissinger: A Biography.* Co-author of *The Wise Men: Six Friends and the World They Made,* he is writing a biography of Albert Einstein. He began his career in journalism as a reporter for *The Sunday Times* of London and then *The Times-Picayune/States-Item.* He earned an M.A. in philosophy, politics, and economics from Pembroke College of Oxford University, where he was a Rhodes Scholar.

Mary Helen Lagasse received the Rudolfo and Patrica Anaya Premio Aztlán Award, a national literary prize established to encourage and reward emerging Chicana and Chicano authors, for her debut novel *The Fifth Sun*, which also won the Miguel Mármol Prize, given annually for the best debut work of fiction by a writer of Latin American heritage. Her second novel, *Navel of the Moon*, is due out in 2006. Ms. Lagasse is a native New Orleanian who taught English and Spanish at private schools in Metairie, a suburb of New Orleans, where she lives with her husband.

Bret Lott is the editor of *The Southern Review*, the famous literary journal founded by Robert Penn Warren, at Louisiana State University. Lott also teaches creative writing at LSU. He is the author of the novels *Jewel*, *A Song I Knew by Heart*, *Reed's Beach*, *A Stranger's House*, and *The Man Who Owned Vermont*, and of the short story collections *The Difference Between Women and Men*, *How to Get Home*, and *A Dream of Old Leaves*. His nonfiction work *Before We Get Started* is a guide to writing and the creative process. He has written a memoir, *Fathers, Sons, and Brothers*, and his stories and essays have appeared in numerous reviews and magazines, including *The Southern Review*, *The Yale Review*, and *Chicago Tribune*.

Wynton Marsalis, the most accomplished and acclaimed jazz artist and composer of his generation, is also a distinguished classical musician. Born in New Orleans, he has helped propel jazz to the forefront of American culture as artistic director of the world-renowned arts organization Jazz at Lincoln Center (JALC). He is the first jazz artist to be awarded the prestigious Pulitzer Prize in music for his work *Blood on the Fields*. A recording artist for two decades, he has produced an incomparable catalogue of more than forty outstanding jazz and classical recordings for Columbia Jazz and Sony Classical, which have earned nine Grammy Awards. In 1983 he became the first and only artist to win both classical and jazz Grammy Awards in one year and, remarkably, repeated this feat in 1984. Internationally noted as a music educator, he was named one of "America's 25 Most Influential People" by *Time* and one of "The 50 Most Influential Boomers" by *Life*. A United Nations "Messenger of Peace," he is co-chair of Lieutenant Governor Mitch Landrieu's National Advisory Board for Culture, Recreation, and Tourism and is a member of Mayor Ray Nagin's Bring Back New Orleans Commission.

Charmaine Neville is a singer and recording artist and a member of the legendary New Orleans musical family. Her father is Charles Neville and her uncles are Aaron, Art, and Cyril of the famous Neville Brothers band. She regularly plays in home venues such as Snug Harbor and Tipitina's, and tours both the United States and Europe. Ms. Neville is an inspiring role model because of her volunteer and benefit work on behalf of children, the elderly, and battered women.

James Nolan is the author of the poetry collections *Why I Live in the Forest* and *What Moves Is Not the Wind* and of

Poet Chief: The Native American Poetics of Walt Whitman and Pablo Neruda. The translator of many works by Spanish authors, including Pablo Neruda's *The Stones of Sky,* his work has appeared in many anthologies. A native New Orleanian, Nolan lives in the French Quarter and divides his time between the Big Easy and Spain. He teaches creative writing in both English and Spanish and writes for various Spanish journals.

Stewart O'Nan is the author of *Snow Angels, The Speed Queen, A World Away, Everyday People, The Names of the Dead, A Prayer for the Dying, The Circus Fire, The Night Country,* and other novels, and a short fiction collection, *In the Walled City. Granta* named him one of the Twenty Best Young American Novelists. *Snow Angels,* his first novel, was selected by Richard Ford to win the gold medal for best novel awarded by The Pirate's Alley Faulkner Society of New Orleans in 1993, an award he credits with helping him get his first book contract. A native of Pittsburgh, O'Nan lives with his wife in Avon, Connecticut.

Paul Prudhomme has propelled the distinctive cuisine of his native Louisiana into the international spotlight and continues to push the limits by creating exciting new American and international dishes. In July 1979, he and his late wife opened K-Paul's Louisiana Kitchen in the French Quarter of New Orleans. Today, it attracts world travelers and continues to excite diners who cheerfully stand in line for a seat in his dining room. He created his own line of food products, including Chef Paul Prudhomme's Magic Seasoning Blends, which are distributed in all fifty states and in more than thirty other countries. A bestselling author, Chef Paul has written numerous cookbooks. His cooking series includes *A Fork in the Road, Fiery Foods That I Love,* and *Chef Paul Prudhomme's Kitchen Expedition.*

Julia Reed is a senior writer at *Vogue* and a contributing editor at *Newsweek.* She also writes a food column for *The New York Times Magazine* and has written the foreword to two recent cookbooks, *The Great American Writers Cookbook* and *The New York Times Chicken Cookbook.* A native of Greenville, Mississippi, Reed lives in New Orleans and is the author of the essay collection *Queen of the Turtle Derby and Other Southern Phenomena.*

Christopher Rice is the author of *A Density of Souls,* which was published when he was twenty-two years old and became a *New York Times* bestseller. His other books include *The Snow Garden,* which received a Lambda Literary Award and, most recently, *Light Before Day.* A columnist for *The Advocate,* Rice lived in New Orleans until recently and now lives in West Hollywood, California.

Harry Shearer is a writer, actor, director, and musician, and a co-creator of *This Is Spinal Tap.* A frequent contributor to National Public Radio, his is the voice of more than a dozen characters on *The Simpsons*. His first comic novel, *Not Enough Indians,* is scheduled for publication in the fall of 2006. He and his wife, composer, singer, and recording artist Judith Owen, divide their time between the French Quarter and Santa Monica.

Ron Shelton, an Academy Award–nominated screenwriter and director, divides his time between Los Angeles and New Orleans, where he has a residence in the French Quarter. His films include *Blaze,* a retelling of the notorious love affair between Louisiana's late Governor Earl Long and Bourbon Street exotic dancer Blaze Starr, *Tin Cup, Bull Durham,* and *Cobb.* His essays have appeared in *The New York Times* and elsewhere. He is married to the actress Lolita Davidovich.

Barbara Boggs Sigmund died at age fifty-one in 1990 after an eight-year battle with cancer. She played in the halls of Congress, wrote letters for President John F. Kennedy, and danced with President Lyndon B. Johnson at her wedding to political science scholar Paul Sigmund. Daughter of Corinne "Lindy" Boggs, a former Democratic congresswoman from Louisiana and U.S. ambassador to the Vatican, and the late Hale Boggs, Democratic majority leader, Sigmund was, first, a member of the town council of Princeton and later twice elected Princeton's mayor. She is much admired for her bravery and humor and charm, for her open discussion of what it was like to face cancer, and for continuing in her leadership roles during her illness. She is the author of *An Unfinished Life*. The Barbara Boggs Sigmund Award is presented annually in her memory by the Center for American Women and Politics, an organization she supported.

Julie Smith is a former reporter for the New Orleans *Times-Picayune* and the *San Francisco Chronicle* who lives in the Faubourg Marigny neighborhood of New Orleans. Her first novel about New Orleans cop Skip Langdon, *New Orleans Mourning,* won the Edgar Allan Poe Award for Best Novel, and she has since published eight more highly acclaimed books in the series. Her most recent novel, *Pi on a Hot Tin Roof,* is her fourth novel featuring African-American New Orleans private eye Talba Wallis, a.k.a. the Baroness Pontalba.

Jervey Tervalon was born in New Orleans and raised in Los Angeles. He is the author of five books, including *Understand This,* which won QPBC's New Voices Award, *The Cocaine Chronicles, Dead Above Ground,* and *Lita.* Formerly the Remsen Bird Writer in Residence at Occidental College, he currently teaches at the Center for African-American Studies at UCLA.

Acknowledgments

My New Orleans would not exist without my agent, Michael Murphy of the Queen Literary Agency, who wanted to do something literary to help New Orleans in the wake of Hurricane Katrina and dreamed up the concept of a book to benefit writers and then sold it.

My New Orleans also would not exist without the generosity of Simon & Schuster, which had already donated considerable funds to hurricane relief before being approached to publish a book to benefit writers. All of us associated with assisting writers are grateful to Simon & Schuster for stepping up to the mark.

My editor, Doris Cooper, gave me difficult guidelines and hard deadlines and provided the balance and encouragement for me to meet them. I am deeply grateful to Doris and to her assistant, Meghan Stevenson, for keeping me on track. The work done by publicist Jamie McDonald on pre-press promotion has been exceptional, and all of us associated with the book are indebted to production editor Tricia Wygal, copy editor John McGhee, and proofreader Aja Shevelew, who all gave up evenings and weekends working on *My New Orleans* so that the project could be completed in record time. Working with the Simon & Schuster team has been a heartwarming experience because each member felt that the book was especially important for the city of New Orleans and its literary community in the wake of Hurricane Katrina.

This book would be as nothing without the words of the contributors, who were willing to give their precious time and talent to help other writers. I thank them for that and, especially, for their cheerful willingness to work with me in achieving a book within the forty days allotted. Communications proved the most difficult stumbling block, with phone lines down and old numbers replaced in the wake of Hurricane Katrina.

I am most grateful for the help given to me by Carol Allen, Jessica Harris, Isobel Allen-Floyd, Shawn McBride, Milton Deckert, Marina Kahn, Randy Fertel, Julia Reed, Harry Connick, David Brinks, Evelyn Maher, and Jackie Clarkson. I am grateful, too, to Cokie Roberts, for making available to us the work of her late sister, Barbara Boggs Sigmund.

In the end, it was my husband, Joe DeSalvo, who made the book possible, reading copy and suggesting revisions, taking on the lion's share of our communal duties to hearth and home and Zuli, our standard poodle, and not complaining about the quality of the food I put on the table while the book was being produced. He did say, just once, that he would be glad when he could have some *caponata* pasta!

Permissions

Spice of Life by Roy Blount, Jr., copyright © 2005 by Roy Blount, Jr., is published here by permission of the author.

This Isn't the Last Dance by Rick Bragg, copyright © 2005 by Rick Bragg, first appeared September 2, 2005, in *The Washington Post,* and is reprinted here with permission of the author.

The Secret Ingredient by Ella Brennan, copyright © 2005 by Ella Brennan, is published here by permission of the author.

Funkytown, or How New Orleans Made Me A Birdwatcher by Poppy Z. Brite, copyright © 2005 by Poppy Z. Brite, is published here by permission of the author.

Mr. Spaceman Arrives by Robert Olen Butler, copyright © 2000 by Robert Olen Butler, first appeared in the novel *Mr. Spaceman,* published by Grove Press, 2000, and is reprinted here by permission of the author.

Our Slow Curve by Leah Chase, copyright © 2005 by Leah Chase, is published here by permission of the author.